To

June & Mac

love

Leonora x

THE
ULTIMATE GIFT -

ELSIE FREDERICK

BALBOA.PRESS

A DIVISION OF HAY HOUSE

Balboa Press books may be ordered through booksellers or by contacting:

Balboa Press
A Division of Hay House
1663 Liberty Drive
Bloomington, IN 47403
www.balboapress.co.uk
UK TFN: 0800 0148647 (Toll Free inside the UK)
UK Local: 02036 956325 (+44 20 3695 6325 from outside the UK)

Because of the dynamic nature of the Internet, any web addresses or
links contained in this book may have changed since publication and
may no longer be valid. The views expressed in this work are solely those
of the author and do not necessarily reflect the views of the publisher,
and the publisher hereby disclaims any responsibility for them.

The author of this book does not dispense medical advice or prescribe the use
of any technique as a form of treatment for physical, emotional, or medical
problems without the advice of a physician, either directly or indirectly. The
intent of the author is only to offer information of a general nature to help
you in your quest for emotional and spiritual well-being. In the event you use
any of the information in this book for yourself, which is your constitutional
right, the author and the publisher assume no responsibility for your actions.

Any people depicted in stock imagery provided by Getty Images are
models, and such images are being used for illustrative purposes only.
Certain stock imagery © Getty Images.

Print information available on the last page.

ISBN: 978-1-9822-8242-4 (sc)
ISBN: 978-1-9822-8243-1 (e)

Balboa Press rev. date: 10/19/2020

CONTENTS

INTRODUCTION

*A*s I have never written a book before I wondered how to start this. How does one make it interesting to the reader, how long should it be, will it make sense and most of all, after all the time it takes to write it, will anyone want to publish it, and, what's more, will anyone want to read this? At the end of the day I have decided that as this is a true story the only way to write it is just to tell it how it is.

I hope that you will find it interesting; some may even find it of some help if they have found themselves in similar circumstances. I might even find that it helps me in the future.

It has taken me over 20 years to write this as so much has happened, some of what we went through at the time has changed now due to improvements in the medical world of transplantation, but the 2020 legal changes to the organ donor scheme make it an appropriate time for me to eventually publish this.

I can only hope with all my heart that eventually this has a happy ending because I do not want to contemplate the alternative. Life is for living, life is now, it is not a rehearsal; we must live and enjoy every day that we have been privileged to have given.

The statistics on heart disease are still frightening. The number of deaths caused each year, how many of the population are affected, the most likely candidates etc. but what you are never fully aware of, until it happens to you, is just how it affects the rest of the family and immediate circle of friends. The trauma and devastation to those closest to the patient can be almost worse than the symptoms of the patient themselves. Of course this applies to any seriously ill person, not just heart disease patients, but the ripple effect onto close family and friends is the same You start looking at other people's shopping trolley and see the junk food loaded in it and watch someone, grossly overweight, eating a plate of chips then lighting up a cigarette and you say to yourself "why did it happen to us?" But then, nobody ever said that life was fair.

What is clear is that we all have a part to play by taking responsibility for our health, some are not so lucky and have illnesses and conditions that no one can change, but for many of us there is a choice. Lifestyle choices, overeating, being overweight, lack of exercise, smoking, excessive drinking, all these factors put enormous strain, not only on our bodies, but on the NHS, and we should not just expect the doctors to cure a situation or condition that we have brought upon ourselves. We need to take responsibility for ourselves instead of the blame culture we live in and expecting someone else to pick up, not just the financial burden, but the ultimate responsibility. For those who find that there is nothing they could have done to change their condition, the doctors will always do their best to try to help; I am eternally grateful to the NHS for what they did to help us.

Part One

BACKGROUND 1988

*W*ell here goes. Where do you start? It must be at the beginning to give you the background and introduce you to the people involved.

In February 1988 I was having a quiet girl's night at my house with a friend who had just returned from a Xmas holiday in Australia. We discussed the usual things like what the kids did over Xmas and how much money we had spent and all the usual trivia, over supper and a bottle or two of wine. A really, pleasant evening but not one that you would have thought would have life changing consequences.

Mel and I had been friends since our early twenties; she had chosen not to have any children and had remained married to her husband when everyone else around her had got divorced. I had been married, had two children, David and Alison, divorced, restarted my career and had established myself as quite happily independent. Not well off but earning enough to buy a modest house, a timeshare apartment in Marbella and, if I was very sensible with money, we managed a ski holiday during spring half term. All in all, I was quite well settled. My office at John Lewis was ten minutes' drive away and my kids were doing well at school.

So, when Mel said "Guess what…….", I didn't realise that my life was just about to change.

The "guess what" was that while she had been away on holiday a couple of their friends who lived locally, had come to the parting of the ways. All divorces, however civilized you try to be, are unpleasant at best. This one was going to rival The War of The Roses, the (Danny de Vito film), but in real life. George's wife had run off with one of his best friends, after having an affair during the previous year with a local farmer whose own wife had gone to stay with her mother taking their 2 girls for a visit over Christmas. Local gossip ran riot about the why's and where fore's of the story as is usual in a small tight knit community but the outcome was that they were getting divorced. Who knows the truth about a marriage break up, lots of surmise and guess work; only the people involved know the truth? Of course there's bitterness and anger, hurt, disappointment and disbelief. That is usually the case, perfectly normal but devastating nonetheless. All this drama was going on in this pretty, sleepy, little village. I hope you have followed all this; it is one of those paragraphs that you might have to read again to make sure you have got it straight in your head.

Anyway, to cut a very long story short, Mel said she thought that I had been on my own long enough, I was having far too much fun being single and that it was time I met someone nice. "You'd like George, he is good fun and good company but feeling a bit bruised at the moment. I will arrange for you to meet each other."

I told her to invite him to dinner the following Saturday (14th). Valentines night is always a difficult night if you are single and unattached, so it had become a tradition whereby I hosted a dinner party at home. Babysitters were always in short supply that night so any singletons could bring their children. The kids could camp out upstairs with my two with games and the tv, popcorn, and snacks, so they had their own party. All my guests, with the exception of Bob and Mel, were single so, as there were going to be a couple of single girls there anyway, it wouldn't look too contrived. The invitation was duly passed on, but I had a phone call from Mel a couple of days later to say that he couldn't come as he had already arranged to go out that night. I thought no more about it until I had a phone call from the man himself. Introducing himself as "George", he thanked me for my invitation and reiterated that he was already going out on Valentines night, but would I like to meet him for lunch as he would be in town the following day? Well - you know, a girl has got to eat and so I agreed. Friday 13th! Time - 1.45pm, place - outside the department store staff entrance, where I worked as the Staff Manager; but how would I know him?

"Easy" he said. "I will be in a navy blazer, white shirt with a red tie and pocket handkerchief and driving a dark green Jaguar XJS."

This is getting more like it, I thought. This sounds promising. When you are single and in your late thirties there are a lot of frogs out there that you don't want to be kissing, but single, smart, good looking princes, driving a supersonic car, are a bit rare.

I met George the following day. His car drew up outside the staff entrance, I got in – what did your mother tell you about getting into cars with strange men? – He looked nice, well groomed, good looking and obviously quite a successful man.

Very promising, I thought.

Lunch came and went, he was very easy going and friendly, quite extrovert and as the hour slipped by we both realised that we had an awful lot in common, kids of similar ages, both owned Great Danes, we all liked skiing and I was a keen follower of motor racing and he was a semi-retired racing driver. I went back into my office and when my secretary asked me if I had had an enjoyable lunch, I announced that I was going to marry him. Not that the lunch was that memorable, nor was it one of those blinding flashes of light, love at first sight or anything like that. I just simply knew.

My Valentine's dinner went very well, everyone enjoyed themselves, dinner was perfect. Bob and Mel spent half the evening, matchmaking by extolling the virtues of George, local racing driver, businessman and recently single. I let them go on for some while then announced, "I met him yesterday for lunch and yes he's very, very nice". That turned the dinner conversation round on its head!

After that I saw George a couple of times for a drink or for lunch but then the kids broke up for half term and I had arranged to take them skiing with a previous boyfriend. When I returned things started to get a bit more involved and during the Easter holidays, we decided that our respective children should meet. George had a daughter and a son, and I had a son and a daughter. Ann was 14 and John was 12. My two were David aged 13 and Alison was 11. I thought that this will be either the beginning or the end of this relationship.

Well, the weekend started well. I took Easter Eggs for everyone and did a massive supermarket shop so there was Hot Cross Buns, yellow candles with Easter Bunny's on them and all sorts of goodies. I felt sorry for George's children. I knew that it was not going to be an easy situation. My kids had had about seven years to get used to living without a father, but Ann and John's mother had only left 3 months before and they were only just coming to terms with their parents' divorce; I was going into their territory to cook a meal in their kitchen, on their mum's cooker. Roast pork and crackling, roast potatoes and all the trimmings, helped to save the day. Its amazing how much teenagers can eat – as if none of them had eaten a proper meal since their mother had left, bottomless pits and it looked like a swarm of locusts had invaded the dining room table. Anyway, everybody got on very well and the weekend was a success. So far - so good, I thought.

Fast forward through the details of the next couple of months, our relationship really had taken off big time and the main points of interest were that the kids continued to get on well, but I was beginning to suffer from exhaustion, both physical and mental. Instead of my old simple life with everything organised to the minute, with my office a 15 minute drive from home and the kids schooling local, I now found myself running two homes, twenty five miles apart, trying my best to cope with a very demanding job, commuting between each end of the East Midlands, washing, ironing, cleaning, cooking and shopping for six of us instead of three and a whole new social life and new friends. Plus a full time career!

I knew that I was burning the candle at both ends and, whilst I know that I am a capable person, I defy anyone to cope with all of that on their own. I am not superwoman, although I would like to think I was. I discussed with George the possibility of his getting a full-time housekeeper/nanny for John and Ann, but even that would not get around the commuting back and forth problem. David had got to an important stage of his education, having to choose his options for his GCSE's and Alison was just about to finish junior school and to start at a new school in the September. So, with all this going on we decided that, although a bit soon in our relationship to make momentous decisions, we would have to all live together, it was the only way to make things work.

George was of the Victorian school where he did not want his wife/partner to go out to work for another company, only his business, and I was of sufficiently old morals about living with someone you were not married to, particularly with teenage kids to be responsible for and set a good example to. So, with much compromising and discussion, in the end we decided that we would all move into George's home, I would leave my job, which was a monumental decision, to give up my salary, pension rights, ability to financially manage my own affairs and home, so I entrusted our lives and livelihood to George. The kids could then all go to the same schools and if all went according to plan, we would get married the following spring. I then took up the role of George's accounts/office manager - just in case I became in danger of having two minutes in a week that I could call my own.

I told you that having supper with Mel was a life changing evening!

The only fly in my otherwise new and exciting life's ointment was Ann. George's daughter, was the eldest of the four. From the outset she made it abundantly clear that did not like me. It took me a while to realise that it would not have mattered who it was that married her father. She was there to make my life as difficult as possible. Her mission in life was to break up our relationship at all costs. It was part of her nature. Quite understandably, she wanted her familiar, old family life back to how it was before the divorce. It is human nature and she was only 14.

I though, was determined that nothing was going to stand in the way of my newfound happiness but however hard I tried over the next 25 or more years, our relationship was never going to be close.

Believe me when I say I tried, boy, did I ever try.

Remember the last paragraph for later in the story.

Ann had always been difficult. She had been since the day she was born; I was reliably informed by both her family and friends. She had never been disciplined by her parents and she did not intend to be disciplined by me. She was wilful, scheming, underhand, selfish and spoilt. What Ann wanted, Ann got, by hook or by crook. She used the situation of her parents' divorce to her advantage on many occasions and just enjoyed making life difficult for the rest of us. We were destined never to get on.

I remember one Saturday evening, before I had given up work. I arrived home at about 7pm having done a day's work and just driven 25 miles back to my new home. I was revving myself up to a very long, ice-cold gin and tonic before I had to cook dinner for the family. As I drove into the farm, a taxi passed me going the other way. I just glimpsed 3 young ladies in the car as they vanished around the corner. I walked indoors to find George, anticipating my need for a drink, pouring tonic into sparkling cut glass, ice cubes crackling as the effervescent liquid poured on top of a generous measure of gin. Oh, how I was ready for that! "Who was that just going out as I came up the drive", I enquired. "Oh, that was the girls. They are off to Roller World for the evening. I said we would pick them up at 11pm. Ann said you were ok with that. There was a ghastly silence and then quietly I managed a controlled reply "Perhaps it would have been a good idea if you had rung me at work to ask me if I would allow my 11 year old into town on a Saturday night until 11 pm!!!." Where was the man's common sense, I wondered? "I'm sorry, George, but that is not on, not suitable, acceptable and not allowed." I said, as politely as I could manage. I put down my drink, walked out of the door and went back to the car. "What about dinner" I heard George shout from the door "and where are you going?" "To town, to bring my daughter back home and you could start dinner whilst I'm gone." I replied, still very controlled. I drove off to go the 11 or so miles, tired and by this time incredibly angry. What I was not prepared for was the sight of my 11-year-old daughter when I finally found them. She had been dressed up in Ann's clothes. At 11 years of age, Alison normally wore appropriate fashionable and trendy clothing but not suitable for the high spots of teenage town on a Saturday night. She was grossly attired in a red leather mini skirt and matching bomber jacket, wearing a pair of Ann's black 3-inch stiletto heeled shoes, her long hair piled up on top of her head and her face complete with full war paint. Red lipstick, mascara, blusher - the works. I was horrified. The controlled smouldering erupted, tiredness and anger took over. I exploded at Ann and her friend. Alison was unceremoniously bundled into the car. Ann did not want to come home with me as she said that she was allowed to be out and so I left her and her friend there and drove home. Poor Alison got the brunt of my temper, tears and upset from us both but the message went home. She did as I said, not what Ann cooked up, and I would not allow my discipline to be undermined in future. That episode created the first row between George and I over Ann's behaviour, the first of many.

Ann was determined to follow her own destiny. She continued to behave badly, attention seeking maybe but I think just devious and naughty. She forged notes with my signature excusing her from school until it emerged at the end of term that she had been absent more than she had attended at her expensive private school., That resulted in her expulsion, then later, at the local comprehensive, caught drinking Vodka out of an orange juice bottle on the school field. We found the brandy decanter at home was being drunk but diluted with water to disguise the level which initially I suspected as the cleaning lady having a little tipple. I found bags hidden at the back of her wardrobe which had obviously been stolen as the security tags were still attached. I confronted her and she was furious that I had been" prying" in her room – I'd actually been hanging up and putting away her clean laundry! I said that I would not tell her father or the police if she promised to return the goods to the shop, I said just leave the bags on the shop floor, no one needs to know. The bags disappeared from her room but I'm not sure if she took them back or not but a couple of days later I found 4 items missing from my jewellery box. I asked her if she knew where they were, but she just stared at me. Revenge! That was her punishing me for the "shoplifting" episode. I have no proof she took them but there was no one else in the house ....? Pranks, maybe but there is within her a hatred, a greed and jealousy. She bought a cheap copy of the gold puzzle ring I bought for George as a wedding ring and wanted him to wear it instead of my ring! She gave George a framed glamour photos of her taken as a 16 year old, in very revealing, inappropriate clothing - actually in very little clothing at all. All very disturbing and I was very worried about her mental state. There are many more tales and stories I could tell you about that would make your hair curl. There is almost another book there, but some things are just better left unsaid. I think you have got the picture of the treacherous character I was dealing with, even in one so young.

She left school at 17 with a couple of mediocre GCSE's. She went to work in a hairdressing salon, then onto a cosmetics company which she left because she found another job on a beauty counter in a department store, next worked in a bar, followed quickly as a sales assistant in a furniture shop, a season in Greece followed by a year in a nightclub in Tenerife, and several other dubious jobs. She worked for a time as a "hostess" in some expensive and infamous London Night Clubs and I don't want to surmise how she earned a living. She became involved with a famous footballer and ended up being cited in his divorce case after being secretly filmed. Oh dear, she seemed to go from bad to worse. Then in November 1997 she produced our first grand - daughter, Ruby.

You can see that life was made quite difficult for George and I, trying to forge a new relationship, accommodating all the needs of our extended families. Ann decided to go and live with her mother after a year or so after our marriage and we only saw her on a part-time basis at weekends and school holidays. Her behaviour continued to be a challenge throughout but the brunt of responsibility changed from us to her mother and so we coped.

I am however, convinced that all children are badly affected by the trauma of divorce but learn, in time, to get on with life. As long as they are secure in the knowledge that it was not their fault and that both parents continue to provide a loving and supportive role. Their secure family unit, once broken up, gives rise to insecurity, split loyalties and can affect them both physically and mentally, very seriously. Sadly, it happens so often, and on top of all that then learning to accept other partners in their parents' lives is also very hard. Huge amounts of understanding is needed and constant reassurance. Sadly, you don't always get it right, however hard you try.

Ann was not all bad although I have painted a rather bleak profile. She had a great sense of humour, her personality was bigger than her petite stature, and was great fun when she was on form. She liked to be the centre of attention and, despite lots of challenges, we also had a lot of hilarity and laughter with her. She got on very well superficially with all the other kids, so there was never any conflict between the children. David and Ann, being closest in age and the elder two, got on very well. Ann thought that she could influence her new younger stepsister, Alison, which she soon learned that I was not going to tolerate.

*G*eorge's son. When I met George, John was 12 years old. A seemingly quiet lonely sort of a boy who spent his entire spare time playing with his skateboard or taking his radio-controlled car to pieces and making it go faster. I wonder where he got that trait from? I have not told you much about George yet and I do not want to digress, but George had been a very successful racing driver who had designed and built his own racing cars.

So, John carried on in his own little world seemingly unperturbed by the recent monumental events in his short life. Somewhere inside I knew there must be thoughts and feelings about the breakup of his family but to this day he has never mentioned anything about it to me and has never shown any sign of emotion. Some children just keep their feelings inside themselves and bottle them up, not the best way to handle trauma and you expect the pressure valve to blow at some point but with John, it never did. Each person handles things differently. I used to find it quite strange because my own kids were such chatterboxes, and so was Ann, rabbiting on about everything and nothing. Anyway, he seemed to be happy enough and, as long as his life ran smoothly and he was fed regularly, he seemed fine. He was a polite boy, just uncommunicative. The most difficult thing to cope with was his eating habits. He had a very limited palate where food was concerned, to the extent that he would not eat a proper meal. I know kids can be faddy with their food but really, there are limits. Beef burgers, chips, chicken nuggets, pot noodles and baked beans were the extent of his repertoire with cereals for breakfast with the tops off four pints of full fat milk or, better still, a jug of single cream. The worst was roast potatoes, cut open with a great dollop of butter on top. Fat on fat. I don't think a green vegetable had ever passed his lips and a fruit bowl was not even in existence in the house.

Now I am not what you would call difficult. I like to think that I am quite easy going and I try to accommodate people's likes and dislikes, but I could not get him to eat anything else. I was used to cooking an evening meal and expecting my family to sit down and eat it with an exchange of the day's news and gossip, school test results and who said what to whom. You know usual family stuff at the end of the day. Communication time they call it, I think! Mealtimes with John were like a battleground at first. It was the only time he was rude." I am not eating that muck "I was greeted with on one occasion when I dished up dinner, "I'll have some beans". "No, you will not" I said, "You'll eat the same as everyone else. I cannot start cooking a different meal for you or everybody will want different food. We sit down as a family and share a meal." "We used to have what we wanted, and we ate when we wanted in front of the TV. Why do we have to wait for Dad and eat at the table? We always have to miss "Neighbours", was the response I got. And so, it went on. Learning to compromise, yet not betray my beliefs about how kids should behave and how to bring them up.

Somewhere along the line we managed, but it is not easy taking on someone else's children and certainly not for the faint hearted. Take heed anyone contemplating it, you need the patience of a saint.

By and large though, apart from the eating problems, we rubbed along well enough. As I said previously, as long as he did the things that he wanted, life with John was peaceful enough. At least he did not cause any havoc to the household and when Ann went back to live with her mother, George assumed that John would want to go too. But he did not. For his own reasons he preferred to stay with us. George never really understood why, but he was thrilled that John wanted to remain with us. He steadfastly stayed with George and I until 1996.

One of the best things about the new arrangement was that the kids all got along like a house on fire, particularly John and Alison. They hit it off from the very beginning. They were all great levellers for each other. If one got a bit uppity then the others put them firmly in their place. Perhaps that was another reason why Ann didn't stay - she was not the sole focus and centre of attention anymore. We had a rota for "chores" like washing up, table laying etc and it was amazing how John always went missing when it was his turn. Alison used to give him lots of grief about that. He always, amazingly, needed the toilet when he was needed to wash up! We used to roar with laughter at how long he took in the shower, "what are you doing in there, you'll be late for school", I seemed to permanently shout. Even funnier was that after spending for ever in the bathroom, the towels were always dry! Just fun times and lovely memories. His skateboard and his radio controlled cars were his life.

Anyway, John continued to race his model cars and still does so now. In all the years I have known him you can count the number of Sunday car meetings that he has missed on 2 hands. He's grown up into a lovely young man with nice manners and a great sense of humour (despite going through the gorilla phase when they only communicate by grunts). He finished an apprenticeship with Rolls Royce and then worked for a company that manufactures model, radio-controlled racing cars.

I had a very good relationship with John, all things considered. Did he have a close relationship with his own parents? Not really, so, using that as a benchmark, it could be classed as reasonable as far as stepmothers / stepsons go.

DAVID

*M*y son. Where do I start with David, and briefly, so as not to bore you with fond mother ramblings?

A delightful baby, but very challenging; he did everything too early, he held his head up in the pram long before the baby books said, he sat up too early, rolled around the floor long before a baby should be able to. Crawled upstairs before I really realised he could crawl and walked, unaided at 11 months climbing on and off the rocking horse he had for his first Christmas, by himself. He could pole vault over the sides of his cot and play pen. Talk about a learning curve as a new mum! He had a great appetite for grown up food, was bored very early on with bland baby rice. He became a delight to feed, never faddy. He loved chillies, curries, Chinese, steaks, anything. He was a skinny kid (he burnt all his calories off in nervous energy), always either on a skateboard or bike. Within seconds of being dressed in clean clothes, he seemed to attract mud. Always with grubby knees, socks at half-mast and with dirty hands, he was definitely hyperactive. However he was also very asthmatic and gave me some terrible scares with his attacks and he spent a fair bit of time in and out of hospital, always very tolerant about things like drips in his arm and injections. He loved to play sports being particularly good at running and skiing (fresh, unpolluted mountain air perhaps?). Later, he became good at rugby, but also he was very good at swimming and water polo. Sometimes though, if the weather was damp, he would collapse, gasping for air and his inhaler, at the side of the football pitch and so he came in for his share of taunting at school. Kids are cruel to each other when they are slightly different to the rest. There is no room for individuality at a young age. You have to be one of the pack. Is it something to do with old animal instincts still within our so-called civilisation? He was no mamby – pamby though and fought back. Too much sometimes and on several occasions, I have had to go to the headmaster because David had been fighting. No bad thing really, he learned to stick up for himself quite early on.

He was (and still is) highly intelligent with a quick wit and mind. Always guaranteed a laugh and never a dull moment with David around. You never knew what he would get up to next. The biggest problem we had with David was channelling that intelligence. "Why do I need to learn my spellings? It is wasting your time and mine. By the time I am grown up, mum; computers will do it for you." I could never get him to understand my reasoning because he always had his own theory. You could not get him to commit words to paper although it was always there in his brain. He was a teacher's worst nightmare - having a very bright child who already knew what was being taught. We just about drilled an education into him, but it was hard going. He managed to twist every teacher round his little finger with his charm and when it came to excuses as to why he had not done his homework – well he wrote the book. I have never heard such tales, always credible, but total fantasies. The truth was that he had forgotten, totally unimportant in David' scheme of things. I sent him to boarding school at the age of 10, not to send him away from home but in desperation and my wits' end that a stricter educational regime may be the answer to getting the best out of him. I wanted to do the best for him and a phrase I have often used in the past springs to mind. "Children don't come with instruction books; you have to bring them up in your own way, using your own guidance and conscience." I have always known how bright David was and feared that lack of stimulus was part of the problem. He did not like being away from home, understandably, but I think that not being able to get away with so much played its' part also. Somehow, he came out of school with a creditable 10 GCSE's and 2 "A" levels and went to university.

David has always been a bit of a "one off" and definitely very individual. My greatest wish is that he could find a career that will challenge and use his doubtless skills to realise his huge potential. When he gets a bee in his bonnet, he is passionate about his subject and will research it thoroughly. He is incredibly well read. I remember when he was at prep school, the headmaster, (and a family friend) rang me up to ask permission for David to read the books from his personal library, because, he said, David had come to him saying "Sir I've read all the books in our library, please can I read yours on mountaineering?" He can converse on subjects that I have no clue about. He got really quite cross when he took an IQ test at school, then gave it to me to do and I got a higher score than him. His housemaster was impressed at my score and entered me to sit the Mensa Test, which I did and was accepted. A permanent source of amusement between us from the past.

Anyone who knows David well would agree that lovely as he is – his brain is always exploding with ideas and views, some a bit off the planet. He ought to be an inventor or a professor, amazing with technology. When he was 6 I bought a Spectrum ZX computer, one of the first home computers. I told him that we would learn how to use it together. By the time I had learned how to switch it on, he had programmed a clock face which changed colour each time the minute hand ticked on to 12. I was a lost cause after that. Ah well it takes all sorts. I know that he will always be a source of anxiety to me, I think your children always are, however old they are. He will never be conventional but as long as he is happy then I will be too.

He has his own house, is a self-admitted coffee addict and lives with the most spoilt cat in the world. He spends an inordinate amount of time on his computer, but I know he is more intelligent than anyone I have ever met, quite frighteningly so.

ALISON

$\mathcal{W}$ hat a joy. You know the old nursery rhyme about sugar and spice, well that could have been written for her. She was a delight as a baby, never kept me up in the night. She sat demurely and played with her toys, never got into trouble at school, always seemed to be as clean at the end of the day as when she had started. Sounds boring but she was not at all and after the traumas of David' childhood, she was a revelation. She has a lovely disposition and manner, always popular at school and, although not as naturally gifted academically as David, she has achieved a far higher level of education and qualifications by sheer hard work and determination

Alison discovered ballet dancing at nursery school and took to it like a duck to water. Before I knew it, I was committed to every Saturday morning, to about 5 different dancing classes. Cost me a fortune back then, but worth every penny. When she was 10, she was selected to dance in the Nottingham Theatre Royal's annual pantomime. That was quite a good description of how the next few months were. Pantomime - juggling act maybe. How do you get to be in 3 different places all at the same time? I spent hours driving back and forth, picking her up from a rehearsal, dropping her off for a performance, somewhere along the line I was also going (trying) to work, shopping, and organising the school run as well as looking after David. Life was hell for 3 months and at the end of it, Alison suffered a case of complete burn out. It had been too much, too soon. She refused to go back to formal dancing classes.

I could have killed her on the spot, but she was adamant that she was not going back. All those years of expense and commitment, still she would not budge. So, I gave up trying to persuade her and let her get on with what was left of her childhood. She continued to be very keen on acting at school and had just landed the part of Joseph in the end of term production of the Amazing Technicolor Dream Coat, when I met George. That was, then, her turn to want to kill me because we were due to move to Derbyshire as she was about to make her stage debut. She had fought with the drama teacher to let her have the part and had won because her singing was better by far, than any of the boys and I then let her down by moving her. To say she was disappointed was an understatement of monumental proportions. In the end she accepted the inevitable with remarkably good grace. If it had been me, I think I would have made a lot more fuss.

Anyway, she progressed through her teenage years with a string of male admirers and a lovely crowd of girlfriends. She enjoyed school and took a highly active part in everything going on including all drama productions and concerts. She still sang at every opportunity and danced, though no formal lessons were entertained. When she finished her GCSE's, she announced that she wanted to go to Nottingham to study for A levels at Clarendon College for Theatre Studies and Dance. How can you turn a kid down when they have worked so hard to achieve their goal? The answer is that you cannot. It meant leaving home at 16 (nearly 17) as it is too far to travel. I felt torn from the inside out, as if I had lost part of me. The umbilical cord was not being untied gently;

it was ripped from me and took a long, long time before the pain subsided. Why did it affect me so badly? Why hadn't I felt glad for her like I did for David when he went off to University? I felt with David that the world's opportunities were out there for him and I wanted him to take them. I was proud of him and, like all mothers, concerned about him going out into the big, bad world but I was ready to push him gently out of the nest. Not so with Alison. I was unreasonable, not to her face (she did not know how I felt) but with myself. I felt lost and without purpose to my life. Deep down I knew she was emotionally quite fragile and maybe too young to be on her own, but she wanted to follow her path.

Time, I thought to go back to work. Give myself another aim in life.

She finished college. Had a couple of fill in jobs before landing a job taking drama workshops into schools all over Nottinghamshire. She loved the work. She can use all her acting and dramatic skills whilst trying to make children aware of various issues that can affect their lives, drugs, teenage pregnancy, domestic violence to name just a few. She feels that she really can make a difference and therefore gets huge satisfaction from that. She will always be an actress. She has an artistic nature that plunges her from highs to lows and back again just as quickly. She is not exactly what you would call moody, but I can talk to her one day and something will have upset her. I'll spend a couple of days worrying about her and when I speak to her again, she has long forgotten the earlier trauma. She suffered a terrible tragedy, so devastating, when her son, little Oscar died. More about that later. She has matured

23

into a lovely, intelligent, strong woman, true to herself in her work, studying now for a master's degree, bringing up Amelia, my beautiful granddaughter.

I always used to say she was a witch when she was little, on account of her long bony fingers and ability to wither you with a stare that could turn you to stone. She also is an uncannily good judge of character. You could guarantee that if she didn't like someone on meeting them, she would be proved right, those she didn't like would not turn out to be good people. She believes in fairies and has her own very definite sense of style; she would definitely have been one of the beautiful people had she been born in San Francisco in the 60's. She is the kindest, most loving and caring person in the world. Self-effacing, never quite believing in her own ability but she has very strong beliefs about what is right and wrong. She and David might be brother and sister, but they are also the best of friends and look after each other. Perhaps I didn't do too bad a job as a parent? Not sure if I should take the praise though, we all develop in our own way.

I quote again a phrase from the last paragraph – "Children don't come with instruction books, you just have, as a parent, to do your best!"

GEORGE

*H*aving met the kids now let me introduce you to the hero of the story. I have got to call him a hero because he is. There are not many people in this world that have gone through what he did and, despite all his ill health, achieved so much.

George, one of five children, left school with an unremarkable school record. He joined the GPO (British Telecom to those aged less than 40) as a Post Office engineer. He discovered motor racing at an early age and spent most of his spare time designing, building and racing his cars. As he became more and more successful, he made the decision to give up his day job and set up a car sales business to support his racing. By this time, he was married to Susan and they ran a very good business and he raced for close on to 20 years. When his wife decided to leave, they had been married for just over 20 years and were comfortable financially. I do not know whether George already had a heart condition in those days. Nobody knows. Was it the stress caused by his wife leaving causing mayhem to a seemingly settled life or was it years of bodily abuse, adrenalin pumping on a racetrack, too much socialising, drink and rich food? It is an impossible question to which there are no answers. When I first met him, he appeared be perfectly normal except when he spoke to his ex-wife on the phone usually to discuss the divorce and what she wanted as a settlement. That resulted in George going bright red in the face, shaking all over and needing a large whisky afterwards. Normal, you might say for someone going through a divorce. There are thousands who go through stress of a similar nature every day and do not end up with the medical problems that George had. His personality was such that he liked to do things his way without compromise, hated to be challenged and in his own view he was always right. Maybe this single minded and selfish persona was what made him so successful as a racing driver. There was no other thought of him being other than "on pole position" but when having to agree to divorce terms, he was never going to accept any of it with good grace. As I have already said earlier, the diet in the house was not good - no fruit, few vegetables, very rich sauces and a lot of meat and cream. I still think that it was a great factor. Having said that, by the time George was first taken ill we had been together 18 months or so and the food regime was quite different. Whatever the reasons diet, genetic, stress, racing or maybe just life in the 20th century, we found out the hard way that George was ill.

We married on 27th May 1989. George had been, not only running a car sales business but, had also become a property developer as well, renovating his Georgian farm and turning the outbuildings into houses. We bought a new (very old) property for us all to live in and bring up the 4 kids, with the adjoining barns for George to convert. It was an idyllic place, like living in a fairy glen, nestling at the bottom of a hill surrounded by woods and fields with 7 springs meeting just below the farm. The house was fairly run down having last been overhauled in the 60's with orange walls in the kitchen and avocado bathroom suites. We set too and made the house lovely - took all the kids out to choose curtains and colour schemes for their rooms and duly made our home together. If anyone can remember what happened to the property market in the late 80's they will understand what happened next. George still had 4 properties to sell at the previous development, and we had borrowed a lot of money to buy the farm. Almost overnight the property market crashed because of the meteoric rise in interest rates. Coupled with the amount of money George had paid out for his divorce settlement only the year before, suddenly we had a huge financial crisis on our hands. We had to borrow the money to develop the barns at enormous cost, then to find that we could not sell the ones we had already got. To compound the problem, the second hand (and new) car market was as dead as the proverbial Dodo. This is the real meaning of stress. All through 1990 we juggled and worked to try to keep everything together. Holidays were not an option but nevertheless we had a particularly good life. Designer trainers were top of the kid's birthday lists but somehow, we managed to persuade them that there were other things more important in life. We got by; however, George was feeling the strain, more so than we realised.

During the summer of 1990 George had a strange episode one Sunday morning, which with hindsight should have been a major warning. He woke up and as usual went to the village to get the papers. When he got to the village shop, he realised that he could not speak. He just picked up the Sunday Times, handed over the money and left. When he got home, I was cooking breakfast and was astounded when he came into the kitchen and just shook his head mouthing words but nothing come out – not a sound. I was scared and immediately called the emergency doctor.

The doctor on call was not our usual GP but he said that if we went straight to our local surgery, we could meet him there rather than wait for our turn on his visiting list. That is what we did. I dropped George off at the surgery and drove straight to school to pick up both boys from Church. (they were day boys at the local boarding school but had to attend school Church on Sunday morning) When I returned with the boys to pick George up, I managed a brief word with the doctor who assured me that nothing was seriously wrong. He thought that George had a facial spasm or palsy and that his speech would return during the day. It did, slowly, and by the evening it was almost back to normal. I suspect now, with the benefit of experience and hindsight, that it was much more than a facial spasm and more likely to have been the signs of an impending minor stroke, too long ago now to be questioned but looking back the signs were all there. It was just that George was a bit too young at 46 to consider that option. I think it niggled in the back of my mind, but you assume that the doctors would know better than you. I say that because later in the story I realise that in George's case, too many errors and mistakes happened because, in part, we did not question the so-called experts enough.

When you lead busy lives, events like that are quickly forgotten and because his speech returned to normal, it did not rate highly in the priority order. It would have done if the problem had continued but by the following day it had almost been forgotten and so the warning was ignored.

The summer turned into autumn and the stress of the overdraft, housing market collapse, motor sales business on its knees was palpable and George looked tired and drawn but he continued to work hard at trying to juggle everything to survive. He was determined to get back on his feet financially and trying to hide the reality from me and the children. Ann was learning to drive, being the eldest and so in September her lessons started, and George took her out for practice sessions at the weekends.

*I*n November 1990, one Monday morning, George went out at 8 am to see the builders as usual, came in at about 8.45 for breakfast. I put his coffee and toast in front of him and went back to the kitchen. Suddenly aware of a strange sound I turned around to see him collapsing onto the floor. I ran and helped him up and into a chair. I had never seen anyone have a heart attack before, but I knew instinctively what it was and how to recognise it now. He was a grey, chalk like colour, like alabaster, the skin almost translucent. He was sweating, not a clammy sort of sweat, but pouring, dripping from him. His shirt was totally soaked through. He was sick, but surprisingly, not in too much pain. I phoned the doctor who told me to phone the ambulance and he would be there as soon as he could. I phoned 999 and they were brilliant, talked to me the whole time whilst relaying the symptoms to the crew who were on their way. Doctor Freeman, our GP arrived minutes later and took control. He gave George an injection to minimise any heart muscle damage done by the attack and was there to greet the ambulance crew who arrived very promptly. It took precisely 10 minutes for the doctor to get to us and 15 for the ambulance, considering that we lived in the wilds of the Derbyshire countryside, they were remarkably fast, for which I was so grateful. George was duly assessed and put into the ambulance to be taken to the local hospital. I followed behind. It is all so clear in my mind that it could have been yesterday and yet it also seems like it was all a dream. You go through things like this fully conscious of what is going on but almost detached mentally. Once in intensive care and stable, I then had to gear myself up to take control of the situation. Made a mental list of what needed to be done: -

1) Phone Mum. At that time, she lived in Hertfordshire, about 100 miles away. Mum and Dad packed a bag and were at my home before Alison got home from school.
2) Rang school and go to see the boys, they were at school and only a couple of miles away.
3) Rang Ann at work and arranged to pick her up after work to take her to the hospital.
4) Rang the builders to make sure they didn't need anything.
5) Rang the car showroom to tell the manager, what had happened and see if he needed anything, could he take over and make decisions for himself for a while.
6) Must ring George's mum - no don't ring, she is an old lady and will panic. Go and see her.

Suddenly, I was rushing around like a whirling dervish organising everything and everybody. I did not give myself a minute to absorb the implications or even think. Please note, this was before we all had mobile phones!

The next few days were mostly spent trying to sleep, shower, dress, eat and get to the hospital in between phone calls. My parents were wonderful as always doing all the ordinary things like washing, ironing, shopping and cooking. Just keeping the home ticking over. The phone became public enemy number 2. From 8 in the morning it would start and then it would just not stop ringing, some days it was 10 or 11am before I could get showered and dressed. The phone calls were amazing. George had a wide circle of friends, family, business colleagues, Round Tablers' and old racing soul mates. The news spread like wildfire and they all rang and wrote. The phone calls, however, drained me. So many people were devastated by the news. They were distraught. I became a councillor to them, reassuring them, keeping them up to date, I had to make a rota of visitors – not too many and not for long so as not to tire George, but they clamoured to see him, all offering help, what can we do? Not wishing to appear rude or ungrateful to so many people offering so much, I said mostly no, as everything was under control when what I wanted to say was "get off the bloody phone so that I can deal with my life" It was exhausting and I couldn't get on with doing everything else. I needed a telephone receptionist.

Dad hit on a wonderful idea, bless him. Buy an answer phone and put an updated bulletin report on George's health every morning and then I did not need to answer it at all. So simple, so that was Dad's mission, to go shopping for an answer phone. Technology, even back in 1990, where would we be without it?

I have said that the phone was public enemy no.2. The number 1 slot was dealing with the relationship between George and his ex-wife. I have not touched much on that side of our life and I don't wish to dwell on what was George's past. To be honest I didn't know much about her in the early days of our relationship; she just figured as the "ex" who had abandoned her children and had gone to live with a farmer in the next village. It had been a classic subject for village gossip, a 5 minute wonder till something more salacious replaced it and something more worthwhile talking about and the focus shifted. As our life together began to settle down, there was plenty of stress and hassle over divorce settlements and "who was having what" from the house. The telephone rows were monumental (I used to pour George a glass of whisky if they had been on the phone for over 5 minutes). He was grey, drained and shaking when he came off the phone. As you can probably understand, I was not impressed but these are the things that have to be dealt with during a divorce. I didn't have a high opinion of her, but I didn't know her and my early overtures to become at least acquainted with her, for the sake of her children, who were, at the beginning, living with us was not well received. In fact I was told less than politely to f… off. I was bearing most of the day to day responsibility for them, but she sneered down her nose at me as if I were the paid help. It was rumoured in the village that I was some sort of a "gold – digger". I wonder who started that? Well, the way things were going, there wasn't going to be much gold left to pan. What with the settlement and legal fees? Anyway, I digress.

When George was rushed into hospital you may remember that I had made a list of things to do. Number 3 was to ring Ann. She was doing a YTS course at a cosmetics shop. I rang her and told her what had happened and told her that I would pick her up after work (the intensive care unit had asked for no visitors during the afternoon to give George chance to rest and for them to monitor him) to take her to the hospital to see her Dad. I had not panicked her and had calmly reassured her that he was fine and stable and would be OK. She, of course, immediately rang her mother. Absolutely understandable, I know. I had then gone to the boys' school to see them, talk to the housemaster about the implications and had collected John, en - route to fetching Ann. When I got to the friend's house where she was staying, Susan came screaming out of the house like a woman possessed. Yelling at the top of her voice in the street she shouted at John, "Your Dad is ok, don't panic, he's not dead, he'll be ok. I came to school to fetch you, but "she" had already collected you. I've already taken Ann and he's going to live". Totally out of control, bawling like a banshee, she tried to open the car door to pull John out. Fortunately, he had his seat belt on, so I just said, quite calmly to her, "Please get out of the way, there is no need for this display. You are not helping the situation and there is no need to panic John". She stopped dead in her tracks just long enough for John to pull the car door shut and I drove away, leaving her screeching down the road. I have to understand her position that she wanted to get to see George with both of their children before I got there but it didn't help George's medical situation - or my state of mind.

So, we arrived to see George, John was relieved to see that his dad was fine. Whilst John was helping himself to the grapes I had bought and flicking the TV remote control, reading the latest copy of Autosport and generally being absorbed by the tubes and drips and associated medical equipment in the ICU room, George quietly turned to me and said "Please don't let Susan in again. Please. She is the last person I want in here. Keep her away, PLEASE." So, I dutifully went to the reception desk and left instructions as to who was not to be admitted, at the patients' absolute request.

The following morning, when I arrived at the ICU ward, I was questioned as to who I was because Susan had previously arrived and told the ICU staff that she was George's wife and it was me who was not to be admitted. I explained to the staff that we were married, and that Susan was the ex-wife, and that George was adamant that he didn't want to see her. He was really distressed because she had walked in, cool as a cucumber that morning, and it had upset him enormously. He shouted at me saying why had I not done as he had asked to keep her away. That was the beginning of an awful 2 weeks, a battle of wits of keeping Susan out. The only people George wanted to see were the children and me. No stress, no business was allowed, just rest and recuperation. Fat chance. I had to be really firm with the hospital staff as to who was allowed in and who was definitely not. I couldn't be there all the time as I had the kids to look after and the businesses to run. Mum and Dad were looking after the day to day running of the house, laundry, cleaning, gardening, cooking etc whilst I was running around like a headless chicken. George just didn't want to see his previous wife at any price. She would pick up her children and take them to visit when she knew I would be otherwise occupied and although she didn't go in again, George of course knew she was sitting outside. Stress, stress and more stress.

I do understand her rationale behind this, it just didn't help George's recovery because he was getting so wound up. That was my main worry and concern.

Despite all of this, gradually, he improved. The

consultant came and went, muttered a few things, words like angiogram, better diet, less salt, less fat, less stress. None of it directed to me, you know, just muttered in passing. I am convinced to this day that I was invisible to him. He never acknowledged me, he simply did not see me, no courtesy to inform me of the situation, no bed side manner, did not discuss the treatment with me. No communication at all. I kept thinking that soon someone is going to explain to me what has happened, what to do next, how this is going to affect our lives etc. Nothing, I was invisible.

After 3 days in the cocoon of an ICU room George improved sufficiently to be released onto the general ward with discharge planned at the end of the following week. George's ex-wife was still going into the hospital, which was damaging psychologically to George, upsetting him all the time and impossible to prevent as there was no visitor monitoring on the general ward. I was by this time getting a little frayed in the nerves department (that was something of an understatement) and I knew that I had got to put a stop to this for everyone's sake.

I wrote her a letter. I pulled no punches. I have never written a letter like it in my life and I hope I never have to again. I explained to her firmly but politely (I think) that she was no longer married to George and that I was. She had relinquished that role of her own volition. I had been looking after her children for the past 2 years and did not appreciate her interference into our lives. I asked her to stay away from George and the hospital, I would escort the children at visiting hours, and would she not come to our home. I told her that she could pick up her children from the end of the drive at a pre-arranged time; you are no longer welcome outside the house as you yell obscenities and throw things at the front door. We had a wood block by the door with the axe that we used for chopping logs for the wood burning stove. In the heat of her temper on one occasion, she had flung the axe at the door. Fortunately, it was so heavy, it didn't get far and landed on the ground but nevertheless, you don't want that sort of stupid behaviour going on. I told her that she was, probably the cause of George's health problems as the stress she had put upon him over the previous 3-4 years was the reason for his heart attack. If he died, she would have the consequences of her actions to live with for the rest of her life. Any more trouble and I would call the police and consult my solicitor. Those are just a few polite excerpts from the letter. It went on for 2 A4 sheets. I showed Mum and Dad the letter and asked their advice. "Shall I send it?" I have always believed in the "least said soonest mended" theory and am normally quite a calm, easy going sort of a person, live and let live attitude, but this situation just could not be allowed to continue. I posted it. I rang a mutual friend to tell her what I had done, I also rang her mother and father. Her parents had seen little of her since she left George. They had supported George and the kids throughout, being very upset with the situation. They had been most kind to me and helped me with Ann and John and indeed my own children. Lovely people, their lives badly affected by the divorce caused by their only daughter. I wanted to exonerate myself for having sent such a vitriolic letter.

I did not need to. The letter hit home, and I had it on good authority later that she was stunned by it. Apparently she was astounded by my audacity. It turned out to be a turning point whereby she finally realised that she had made a monumental error of judgement and it was only the shock of the possibility of George dying that had brought it home. It was too late, he was remarried and not to a bimbo, gold-digger. That I was a half intelligent person who was not going to let her life be controlled by the whim of the "ex" must have been a bitter pill to swallow. As previously said, the letter was long and hard hitting but no more to be recounted here.

I digress again. On the Saturday morning George was due to be discharged. I told you earlier, that George had been a racing driver. His greatest love and passion in the world were his cars. He had always driven a Jaguar XJS amongst many other luxury, performance cars and true to form that is what he had sitting at home in the garage. Having had a heart attack, we knew he would not be allowed to drive for a few weeks, so I thought I would collect him from the hospital in his Jag. Off I set via the car wash so that it was sparkling clean for him. Big mistake. Always convinced that women drivers were not fit to be on the road, George was concerned if I went out in the Jag, careful though I was making sure the aerial was down, windows shut, wing mirrors retracted, I had not bargained on the car wash removing the rear bumper body kit. More panic. Fortunately, the garage owner was on the forecourt and female tears and pleading prevailed. "Please help me, my husband will kill me" I wailed and the proprietor, obviously concurred with George's opinion that women should stay in the kitchen, was anxious to help rather than let one of his fellow species languish in jail for murder. He was also concerned that I might sue him for damages. Anyway, the car was soon as good as new and off I set.

When I arrived, it was obvious that all was not well. George was lying down with his head under the pillow trying to stop the noise of the ward, which was agitating him. I asked the sister on duty what was going on. She was quite short with me, obviously being terribly busy, saying that when the doctor arrived to discharge him, we could ask him then. Apparently, George had told the sister he did not feel well at about 8am and she had called the on-call doctor. Being a weekend there was only one doctor on duty and therefore it was going to be a while before he did his rounds. Do not ever be ill in hospital at weekends – nothing happens till Monday! Three or four times during that day I asked when the doctor was coming and eventually at 8pm the doctor arrived. He immediately had George moved to a side room, called for an ECG and within minutes decided that George had suffered another heart attack right under their noses. I was a deadly cocktail of emotions. Upset, devastated, angry, furious, hopping mad, concerned, confused, tearful – how can that happen in hospital, where was the monitoring, where was the doctor on call, what were they thinking of?

So, back we went to the ICU.

Two weeks later George came home. He was quite frail and pale to start with but soon started to look better although he tired very quickly. We had a lot of support from our GP who I have not yet talked about in great depth, but we owe a huge debt of gratitude to him for his support and care. He suggested ways of looking at our diet, stress management and other factors. Diet was something that I could physically control and monitor. The first change was to ditch the chip pan. I had always been used to eating sensibly, lots of fresh fruit, salad and veg and no ready meals, processed and preserved foods because David was a serious asthmatic and was extremely sensitive to foods with added colourings, e – numbers etc. We avoided Coca-Cola, red and yellow jelly, food additives, pre-prepared meals, Smarties and the like when he was a little boy. He used to have to repeat to me a list of what he must not eat at children's birthday parties before I let him go. I always tried to cook proper meals with fish featuring high on the menu. It was therefore quite easy for me to understand the harm that a diet high in saturated fat and salt could do. I met with a fair bit of opposition, however, skimmed milk was condemned as "grey milk" and low fat spread instead of butter was not well received. It does not matter how good it is for you, you always want what you cannot have. George liked butter on his toast spread thick enough to leave a perfect imprint of his teeth. A dentist could have made a set of dentures from the impression left on George's toast. John liked the top of the milk, several tops in fact, off several pints, on his breakfast cereal so he revolted as well at the new regime. More and more veg appeared on the plates and less roast potatoes – another reason to moan at me and instead of cream buns, puddings and chocolates around the house, more fruit appeared. "Salad – what's that – rabbit food, not eating that? I want a pot noodle" said John. Do you know what really made me cross? All this healthy eating, George's cholesterol level came down dramatically, I am sure the kids were better for it, but I did not lose an ounce of weight! Life is cruel!

As I have said, food I could control. George's attitude

I could not. He rebelled against acceptance that he had a heart condition. When he became tired, he would not let his body rest he just became angry. If things did not go his way in business, he lost his temper. He refused to accept defeat in anything, bank managers, interest rates, national recession, growing teenagers with all their associated problems and hormones, not inconsiderable being as there were 4 of them, declining car sales, non - existent house sales and - me.

Of course, there was me. I became the kicking block for everything that went wrong. It was always my fault. Well, it was bound to be, wasn't it? George did not have a heart condition before he met me, did he? He did not have the stress of 4 children before he met me, did he? He had more money before he met me, didn't he? (The ex had taken the other half!)

OK, I am not perfect, far from it, but I could not take all that responsibility on board could I? So of course I retaliated and for the first time in our married life we started to row badly. I am a very even tempered, easy going, happy go lucky person but we started to argue about everything. George blamed me for every mortal thing. I could not do right for wrong. If I said something was white, he would say it was black. If the sun was out I'd say what a lovely day and George said it wasn't. And so, it went on. Every time we argued George said it hurt his chest and I was to blame. So everything had to be done George's way, no room for compromise or discussion. It was an emotional blackmail situation. In today's world it would be classed as Coercive Control. I went to our local GP, who was supportive and agreed that George was being totally unreasonable but sometimes people with serious conditions have to find a scapegoat for themselves. He had to have someone to blame and would not recognise the need to take responsibility for himself. The doctor suggested some counselling for George to help him come to terms with himself. We went and despite my gloom I had to laugh to myself when George told the councillor that it was me who needed the help, and please would he tell me to stop causing trouble? I know it takes two, but I could not do right for wrong.

During the next 12 months we gradually learnt to live with each other, the situation not really improving but an acceptance on my part that this was how it was going to be, I think, helped. When things got really bad, I went out shopping. Asda, Tesco's, Sainsbury's and John Lewis, anywhere. With 4 kids in the house, food shopping was always necessary. I alternated my trips, had a coffee, glass of wine, took some deep breaths and counted to ten. Then I went back home.

That same year we moved out of our lovely farmhouse into the first of the converted barns, now finished. I was devastated when George said we had to move. I wanted to stay there forever but the fates had decided that a lovely doctor and his wife would find it and buy it from us. We had not sold any of the other properties and this sale would hugely reduce the financial pressure on George. We moved into the barn and it was great fun. The couple who bought our house were then next door with their lovely 3 boys (soon to be 4). We became great friends (and I still am) and became godparents to son no.4.

Meeting Peter and Mandy was a lifesaver, quite literally. Peter was a consultant orthopaedic surgeon, now retired, but back then he had just been appointed from his previous position to a consultant. They had been house hunting for a while when they found one of George's barn conversions advertised for sale. It was not really big enough for their expanding family and so George showed them around our farmhouse. They fell in love with it immediately and George was left with the task of convincing me that we had to move. I knew that we would have to sell because of the dreadful recession that happened in 1990 and we were in such a financially precarious state; the burden on George was immense. So, we moved next door and, as I have said, we all became great friends. We enjoyed curries together, BBQ's in the summer, glasses of wine and the odd G & T! We had built a swimming pool in the garden, so we had great times with their boys and our kids in the pool. With the financial climate looking a bit healthier, George's temper improved, and he was much less stressed.

The VAT office decided to investigate our car sales business. They just arrived on the doorstep one morning. I thought it was the annual check whereby they go through the years books and see if they can find any mistakes. Well I had been doing the books since I met George and although I have said it previously, I am not quite perfect, I kept the books accurately. We are not dishonest people. I am not clever enough to fiddle things and anyway I have never felt the need to defraud anyone – it is not my nature. After about 2 hours of looking at the paperwork I offered this man a cup of coffee. He looked at me and said "I won't be bribed you know" I went into the kitchen and said to George "I think this is a bit serious" - I had never been spoken to like that before and was quite worried. He was there all day. At 5 PM he said that he would be back the following day because he had a lot more work to do. "I'm not finished with you yet" were his words. The following morning, he arrived. George and I had decided the night before that we would leave him to the office to help himself to what he wanted and that I would neither offer coffee or help, but I did say that we had to go out in the afternoon, as George had an appointment with the heart consultant. The office had its own front door but adjoined the house via the kitchen. He was happy to be left alone and said he would lock up and post the key back through the letter box when he had finished. When we returned there was a note from him saying that he had taken certain books to continue his investigation and he had taken the contents of the office litter bin? Strange I thought but when I went into the kitchen, I realised that the contents of the swing top rubbish bin had gone as well. Now I was really cross. This man had abused the fact that we were out and had come into our house. How dare he? It had never occurred to me that he might go through the house whilst we were out. What on earth was going on? If ever anyone has experienced being investigated like that, they will relate to how we felt. Never mind George being stressed, I was furious, scared, I felt almost violated and worried all at the same time. The worst thing was that I had done nothing to warrant that sort of strain. The following day I rang the VAT office to find out how long he needed the books for, as I could not get on with my work. He was vile. He told me that he thought I was very clever but that he would find us out." I'll get you – you can't fool me". So, shaking with rage I told him that I had never been spoken to like that before, that I had done nothing wrong and that he had no right to go poking about in my house. It was an invasion of our

45

privacy. Who did he think he was? I told him that George was a sick man and did not need that sort of harassment and neither did I. When I came off the phone I burst into tears. No man was going to upset me like that. So, I gathered myself and then phoned the VAT office back and asked to speak to the most senior person there was available. I complained bitterly that we were being treated like criminals and I was not going to put up with this behaviour. I received an apology and a couple of weeks later this man rang me and said if we paid what he thought we owed in VAT he would not continue the search. I told him that we would pay whatever was due, but he had to prove to us that we owed it, not just some figure he had plucked out of the air. When you finish your investigation and decide what is actually due you can have a cheque then and not before. In the end it took about 2 years for them to finish their investigations. I woke up suddenly in the middle of the night many, many months later, woke George up and said" I know where the money is". Not popular for waking him up he just grunted and turned over. I got up and in dressing gown and slippers went into the office. From 3am I worked flat out for hours but afterwards came out with a big grin on my face. Oh, how I was going to enjoy the next conversation. I rang the VAT inspector and told him I had found the amount of money that he said we owed. "I knew you'd have to admit your fraud in the end" he said, "you people always do when you know the net is closing around you". You pompous man, oh you don't know what I'm going to hit you with next, I thought "Actually, we don't owe you anything. The VAT rate changed from 15% to 17.5% and you have been assuming that we should have been paying the higher rate but the period you are investigating was before the rate changed. I have spent all night looking at every transaction we carried out during the time you are investigating and the amount of money, almost to the penny, is because you were looking at the wrong time period. We paid the exact amount of 15% which was correct. You are in the wrong and have given us nearly 2 years of stress and grief. I will be reporting you and I will expect a written apology". Amazingly our phone line cut out at that very moment: I have never heard from them again. Did we need that episode in our lives? I don't think so!

George was astonished that I had had the brainwave which solved the problem. I think I went up in his estimation at that point. He proudly went around our friends and told them that I had taken on the might of the VAT and won. We dined out on that success story many times after that.

However George said that he had had enough fighting that sort of battle and it was time to close down the car business and concentrate on the building and property development side. It was more profitable and less stressful.

He declared that never again would he be in a business that required being VAT registered.

HEART ATTACK 3

*1*992 It was some time after Mandy and Peter moved in, we had been telling Peter about George's medical condition. He is an orthopaedic consultant but nevertheless he had a better knowledge of anything medical, especially heart conditions, than us. Peter gave George a lot of advice about his medical condition which George took great note of and one of the things that Peter could not understand was that despite 2 heart attacks, the heart consultant had never referred George for an angiogram. He found it difficult to believe that George could have had 2 heart attacks and not have any follow up treatment other than a 6-month appointment to see the consultant at the hospital and a few pills. Why haven't you had an angiogram? We do not know, do we? What is an angiogram? Why don't you ask the consultant?

We did not even know what an angiogram was. Why should we? It is not the sort of thing the average person knows about unless you are medically trained. Anyway, over a period of months Peter kept on at George about getting this procedure done and eventually our GP rang the hospital and asked for George to go on the waiting list. There are times when, with the benefit of hindsight, we should have paid privately and got him there sooner but that is all history now.

That summer the weather was wonderful. The household was a bit under pressure from kids and exams, (Minor Understatement, more like a powder keg about to blow!!) David was doing A levels; John was doing GCSE's and Alison was choosing options, so a lot was going on but that's normal with a house full of hormonal kids isn't it? I decided to take the kids away in July when school had finished. Susan had booked a holiday for John and Ann, so I suggested taking David and Alison to Spain, each taking a friend. George wanted to come with us but at the point of booking his oldest friend decided to get married in the Isle of Man which somewhat snookered the plans. So, it was agreed that George went to Bill and Jeans' wedding and we went to Spain. Off we all went, and a great time was had by all. I think it did us good to get away from each other and I had the best time. My idea of a perfect holiday at that time was the beach, sun; good books punctuated with regular gin and tonics. The kids entertained themselves and their company and humour was brilliant. There was never a dull moment, great break and much needed rest from the routine of home for us all. I was able to sit on a beach for 2 weeks undisturbed, book in one hand and a steady supply of gin and tonics in the other. I am not an alcoholic but do believe in the relaxation properties of the odd G and T. Kids got up about lunchtime and came to find me on the beach. They stayed out partying till about 4am. No hassle and stress; just what we all needed.

George came to Manchester airport 2 weeks later to meet us. He looked dreadful I thought. Was it the airport lighting that made him look such a horrible shade of yellowing grey or was it that we all looked so tanned? He had had a good time at his friend's wedding, but he definitely looked a strange colour.

The following day George and I went to a friends' birthday party at one of our local pubs. Great party with bouncy castle for adults! What middle-aged people can do after a few glasses of wine is quite scary really. There were 60-year old's doing forward rolls and back flips and George was there in the thick of it. Much hilarity and laughter! Later that afternoon he said he didn't feel too well – did I think it was something that he had eaten? Oh, silly man, I knew that wasn't the reason, I could read the signs. He had gone that transparent sort of alabaster colour again, so I suggested that he went to the hospital, just in case. So, I drove him – big mistake. If you phone for an ambulance they rush you straight into casualty and you are seen – or at least you are assessed quite quickly. If you drive in, you just join the queue. Sunday night in A and E again I have said it before – you do not want to be in hospital at the weekend. By midnight they decided that George had probably had another heart attack, but they would not know till the blood tests were returned. So off we go back to ICU where it was confirmed that he had indeed had a further heart attack, this one more severe than the previous two. One-week later he was discharged, and George came home. This time I could see a huge deterioration in him. He was very weak, very grey and very bad tempered. It took weeks and weeks for him to recover. George would sleep during the afternoon, by the pool wrapped in a blanket whilst the weather was good and as autumn approached, he would go to bed every afternoon. This was not a good time for any of us. I was worried sick.

One good thing was that the financial pressure had eased somewhat with the sales of the final two properties at the old farm development and the sale of the garage showrooms now complete, and our office now just off the kitchen, it meant that George could pop in and out at will. The manager was running things, so George just did the things he liked and left me to do the mundane and the paperwork.

You would have thought that after 3 heart attacks the consultant would have taken this case more seriously and at least talked to us.

No.

Peter continued to give advice to George about having not had an angiogram. I was increasingly annoyed with the lack of treatment and communication from the consultant and together with our doctor's support and letters, we changed consultant, who immediately put George on his list for an angiogram.

That autumn I had been enduring dreadful pain in my feet which Peter diagnosed one evening over a curry with "god, your feet look awful. They need operating on and fast". I had been sitting cross legged on the floor in bare feet. He arranged for me to see a consultant colleague of his who roared with laughter when he read Peter's description of my feet. I didn't think they looked that bad, just very swollen, red, big toe joints. Bunions to layman, bloody painful to me. In fact, I cannot think of a worse pain. They arranged for me to have the wretched things done on January 9th, 1993, David's birthday, to which he said, "great job Mum, that's knackered my birthday plans then". Don't you love kids' ungratefulness? Sadly, many years later I scuppered his 40th birthday plans by having hip replacement surgery on that day as well. Note to self. Must plan better in future???

So off I went to have my feet done. I was home within 3 days with both feet encased in plaster for 6 weeks. Well I thought it is January. I do not want to go out in this weather anyway and my feet will be beautiful for the spring.

Sods law says that I could not possibly have 6 weeks to sit on my backside being waited on with some good books, could I? Too long for her to be idle. I will let her have a few days though. How kind! The following week a phone call from the heart unit at Leicestershire said they would like George for an angiogram the following day. I could not drive for at least 6 weeks. Jason, our car company manager, bless his heart, stepped into the breach and took George, stayed with him overnight at the hospital then brought him back the following day. They had to stay overnight because his artery haemorrhaged, and they had to give him a transfusion. It is never straightforward is it? It must be something bad I did in a past life, I think.

The results came through very quickly. George needed a triple by-pass operation as he had 3 very blocked arteries. The next few weeks were quiet. I was hobbling around in my casts; the weather was very bleak and cold, typical January and February. Then came the day to take off the casts. Well if my feet looked bad before, it was nothing to the way they looked now. More like an injured alligator! Scaly skin, red, green, yellow and purple bruising and swollen to elephantine proportions, with neat rows of black knots. Shoes? don't be silly, not a chance. I didn't think I would ever get a pair of shoes on ever again. What about my vast collection of high heels, racks of them rivalling those of Imelda Marcos? Nothing would go on except George's fluffy slippers and soft socks. Still, Peter assured me they would get better, handing me a glass of gin and tonic whilst giggling uncontrollably.

The weekend that the casts came off was particularly cold. John's car needed attention so there was George lying on the frozen ground, underneath the car trying to mend it.

I told him he was a silly old fool and why didn't a fit young man like John do the tinkering underneath with George giving out instructions but no, of course he knew better. On Sunday, George felt very weak and deteriorated during the day. He was too weak even to lift the kettle to make a cup of tea. He looked grey and old. I sent him to bed early. On Monday morning, he looked no better and so I rang Doctor Freeman. He was at our house by 10am. By ten past ten he was on the phone to the heart unit. He said that George needed to have this by-pass immediately, it was critical, and no excuse would be acceptable, by 3 pm we were on the way, they had a bed for him. Me driving in my soft socks and George's slippers in the freezing depths of winter. True to form George had taken his brief case and mobile phone with him. It was the old fashioned type of phone, looked like a brick with a long aerial and the battery weighed a ton. Anybody coming between George and his business does so at their peril. I dared not say a word for fear of losing my head. Fortunately, Paul, the male nurse on duty, had no such qualms. "We're not going to need these in here are we?" he said "you'd better take them home with you as they will be safer there" firmly taking the brief case and phone from George and giving it to me, at the same time giving George a look that forbad any argument. We got George settled in and examined. ECG's revealed that there was a lot of heart activity and therefore they would need to rest George before any surgery could take place. What they really meant was that he was on the brink of another heart attack and surgery at that point would probably send him into cardiac arrest and could kill him, but they put it in medical terms that I did not quite understand till much later.

HEART ATTACK NO. 4 AND BY- PASS SURGERY

*R*eassured that George was going to rest for a few days and that at long last they seemed to know what they were talking about and were doing something positive, I relaxed. Driving was quite uncomfortable because my feet were so sore, but the hospital was only half an hour away so with the help of good and frequent painkillers I could manage.

It was my Dad's 70th birthday the following weekend. March 5th. He was as fit as a fiddle and full of the joys of spring, he was not aware that we had planned a surprise birthday party for him on the Saturday afternoon. I had arranged to poach and dress a whole salmon, bake a birthday cake and take it to Hertfordshire with the kids. This had been planned for weeks, long before the events of the previous weekend. Lulled into this false sense of calm and confidence, I assured Mum that all would be well; obviously, George would not be there but as far as I knew the party could go ahead as arranged. Mandy stepped into the breech and baked a wonderful cake in the shape of a wedge of Blue Stilton cheese (Dad's favourite) complete with mouldy holes and marzipan mice swarming all over. It was a wonderful cake and would appeal to my Dad's sense of humour. He would love it. The salmon was on order, to be delivered on Friday. I was too organized; I should have known then or at least have a sense of foreboding. Sometimes I wonder how I did all this when I look back. Was someone testing me to see how much I could cope with before I collapsed from total stress and exhaustion? Just what is my breaking point?

So, to recap, Monday George had gone into hospital, on Tuesday they were hoping to operate on Thursday or Friday when they had stabilised his heart activity but by Wednesday, they had a series of emergencies which pushed George back down the priority list. George, not known for his patience at the best of times, was feeling restless and fidgety. He had sat still for the best part of three days and was feeling rested and better. He did not want to stay in hospital over the weekend to wait for possible surgery the next week, he wanted to come home. I wanted him to stay in, as I knew it was going to be a hectic time with the party. Paul, the male nurse in charge of George was kind, but firm, and assured him that he was better off staying put so that they could slip him in for surgery at the first available opportunity. When I left him on Wednesday evening, he was calmer and resigned to staying. I had a dental appointment the following morning so I told Paul that I would be there about lunchtime, then left and drove home. Mandy and Peter really were my mainstays at the time. Every evening as I pulled into the courtyard on my return from the hospital, as I got out of the car a Gordon's gin bottle was waved out of the farmhouse door. As if by remote control, on auto pilot, my feet, still red and swollen and in George's slippers, carried me to their house, even if I was dropping with tiredness, the gin and tonic beckoned. They were great because Peter was able to translate the medical jargon I had been told during the day, into understandable layman's language. It also meant that Peter knew exactly what was going on. Half an hour and two large gins later I was able to go home, phone the boys, mum, mum in law, answer the messages on the answer phone, talk to Alison, a bath and bed. I never have had any problems sleeping; I used to fall into bed and struggle to get up with the alarm. Thursday morning was going to be a respite. I could get up slowly; get Alison off to school and drift quietly through the morning till dentist time. Not the usual race to get to the hospital early because George liked me to get there as soon as possible.

I rang the ward at about 8.30 to see if he had had a good night. Paul came on the phone and said "George wasn't feeling very well earlier this morning, so they have taken him straight to the theatre for his by-pass. Don't rush to get here because he'll be out for a few hours, take your time, go to the dentist and come over this afternoon." I was ecstatic. I rang mum, George's mum, his brothers, sister, everyone. "They have found a slot for him and he's having his surgery now. I'll keep you posted, ring you later." "I'll call and see you on my way home this evening" I told George's mum, knowing she would be anxious.

I went to the dentist, did some shopping for grapes, chocolates, flowers and the obligatory latest copy of Auto Sport and drove to the hospital. I found Paul who pointed me in the direction of the waiting room by the recovery ward. It was about 12.30 in the afternoon when I got to the waiting room and after half an hour I wondered if anyone still knew that I was there. Nobody was about so I found my way to the café, had a coffee and a sandwich and returned to wait. I was on my own for ages before a nurse came in. I asked if she had any news, she went away to find out and came back to tell me that George was still in the theatre so she could tell me nothing. I sat there till 8pm in the evening when, finally, a doctor finally came to see me. He told me that George had been very ill during the night and so they decided to operate straight away. There had been a few complications, but he was now in the recovery room and I could see him briefly. He was unconscious and wired to every machine in the room, drips and wires everywhere. The sister on duty assured me that it was quite normal, but it gave me a shock, nevertheless, to see George like that. He did not move apart from the rise and fall of his chest. He was that strange alabaster colour, almost like a waxwork. It was quickly obvious that George had no idea that I was there although the sister encouraged me to talk to him. I stayed for about an hour by which time I felt emotionally drained and physically exhausted. I had never felt so alone in my life. I was not in control of the situation and neither did I understand what was going on. As I sat there holding George's fingers, his hands were attached to wires, monitors and something that looked like a clothes peg, (measures the oxygen saturation I found out later), stuck onto the end of one finger, I wondered if other people had this feeling of total helplessness. The events of the past few years came back to me and the subsequent implications of the future were something I could not even begin to contemplate. I asked myself if I should have anticipated all this, realised that my complete and utter lack of any medical knowledge had allowed me to accept what little information we had been given by the doctors. I had never even questioned what we had been told and the blinding realization was that we had been given platitudes, not been given intelligent information on which to be able to form any informed decisions. We were almost non-entities in the eyes of the medical profession.

Non-medics do not belong to the elite inner circle; keep the patients and the family in the dark about their condition, then they do not ask questions and make a fuss.

When George had first had a heart attack, he should have been given an angiogram then in order to assess the condition of his arteries. We should have been informed as to the possibility of by-pass surgery and the consequences of delay. Instead we went along with what we were told just like little children or a flock of sheep. Do as you are told, don't ask because you couldn't possibly be intelligent enough to understand that if you abuse your body with bad diet, overload with stress coupled with the very real threat that the whole thing could be genetic and that you should really choose your parents carefully, you could easily have a serious heart condition. I am not really blaming the medics; they cannot be expected to explain to every patient the same story; they simply haven't the time. We were as much at fault. We should have researched the condition more carefully, asked the right questions and perhaps had a second opinion. There was no such thing as a Google search engine back then. If Peter had not commented that he did not understand why George had not had an angiogram. If, if, if.

I realised, as if coming out of a dream that I had to go and see George's mum. The whole of our little world was waiting for news and I must pull myself together and face them. What do I tell everybody? I cannot tell them he is fine – he isn't. The sister tells me that they are keeping him sedated for the time being to let his body heal. "He'll look better in a day or two, dear. See you in the morning" was her cheery dismissal of me.

I went to see the Mum's. George's mum had gone to

relations for the wait, for the company and the comfort. Dinner had been cooked for me, but I was beyond eating. I tried to be cheerful and encouraging. I must have missed my vocation and should have been an actress. I put on quite a convincing performance. The ward sister had told me that the by – pass surgery had been successful and that he would be quick to recover although he looked quite poorly now. Having put their minds to rest I went home. I arrived in the courtyard and true to form the Gordon's was beckoning. Alison was there. She had gone next door for the company and comfort as well. God bless Peter, he put his arms around me and that was that. Floodgates open, those were the first tears I had shed. If I hadn't cried, then I think I would have exploded with the tension. Several large gins later, Alison and I went home to bed. Peter knew from what I had told him that all was not as straightforward as had been made out. I was still unaware of the real crisis that occurred that day. Having said that I wanted to be informed, it was probably as well that I did not know the full story at that moment. I slept like the dead; I was so exhausted I had not even had time to think about the pain in my feet, the worst was the throbbing in my head.

Friday morning came too soon, and I dragged myself up to get Alison off to school. She was a gem. She never grumbled about my absences at the hospital, she just got on with her life, sorted herself out, borrowed dinner money from Mandy, got her own tea, and ironed her uniform. She didn't trouble me with trivia but was always here with a hug. "Hi mum, how's George doing "she'd call out. Thank goodness she was in the house. She was the heart of the house at that time. Anyway Friday, more lists of phone calls, to go to school to give the boys an update on George, deal with the mail, and "oh my god, it's Dad's party tomorrow" as the fish man arrived with a huge salmon for me to poach. Isn't the human body amazing how it can cope with a million tasks at the time of total crisis? Adrenalin – can cause harm if too much but enables you to do the job when needed. So, I poached salmon, dealt with the list of jobs and drove to the hospital. I suppose my mind was so full of things to do that I didn't allow myself to consider what I was going to find at the hospital. Just as well.

George had been moved to the ICU and was still attached to a battery of machines. It looked a bit like the Kennedy Space Centre. Banks of monitors lined the walls all with zigzag horizontal lines streaking across them. Wires, cables, drips with red and yellow bags hanging, and quiet. The quiet, interspersed with the hum of the machines and intermittent bleeps of the drips. Nurses went about their business crisply and quietly. No chatter, even their shoes were quiet on the floor.

There were about eight patients in the ward and George was right at the side of the nurse's station. I asked the questions about his progress, did he have a good night, when was he likely to come around, what was happening? Gradually during the day, I gleaned more information. The sister in charge of George had to check on his levels, temperature, blood pressure, drips, monitors etc. every half hour. It was like painting the Forth Bridge. Just as she finished the last check it was time to start at the beginning again. I sat mesmerized, literally it was "intensive" care. The cost to the NHS must be astronomical to run a ward like that. The level of staff – no juniors here. No one below the rank of sister and one to each patient at least. No nipping off for a quick coffee. As each one went for a break there had to be a complete hand over to another sister and change of shift was run like a military tattoo. As the day progressed, I began to find out the events of the previous day. George had been ill. So ill in fact that at 4 in the morning the man in the next bed had pressed the alarm button. George was having another heart attack. This time it was a major one. He was rushed straight from the ward to the theatre where they operated on him literally to save his life. He was in the theatre most of the day. His heart had stopped, they revived him, completed the surgery and when they tried to get him off the by-pass machine his heart wouldn't go by itself, they worked on him for hours, massaging his heart till it started to beat. When finally his heart started they then couldn't control his potassium level. Slowly it began to sink in that whilst I had been at the dentist and out shopping, doing mundane tasks, George had been fighting the fight of his life. That realisation made me break out in a cold sweat. I was helpless, completely at the mercy of these people. I know that they were doing their best, but I was terrified. Cold, horror struck, for the first time it hit home that George could have died, could still die. He was still out for the count, hadn't even opened his eyes, why? The answer given was that they were still having trouble controlling the level of potassium and that they were keeping him sedated for that reason.

I stayed by his side all day. I couldn't do anything, but I didn't want to be anywhere else. It appeared that they were going to keep him sedated for a day or two, so they suggested that I went home to rest. I went home feeling empty, helpless and pretty damned useless.

Saturday dawned. Dad's seventieth birthday. John was going to his mother's for the weekend. Skin the poached salmon. Slice cucumber and lemons to dress the fish, load into the car. Pack overnight bag for the kids and me, pick up cake from Mandy, pick up David from school, drive to the hospital with the kids, and sit with George all morning, there was no change. I had George's mobile phone and left the number as well as Mum's phone number with the sister in charge, with the strict instructions that if there was any change, they could get me, day or night. I would be back the following morning.

In the early afternoon, we drove to Hertfordshire. I love my Dad very much, but I have never felt less like going to a party in my life. At least the journey gave me chance to talk to David and Alison. They had been visibly shaken at the sight of George and I needed to reassure them, at the same time tell them the truth and the reality of the situation. I am so lucky to have my kids. Perhaps it was because of my divorce from their father – I do not know. We have always had the ability to be honest and truthful with each other. I have always been able to talk to them and, despite their youth, they have always been understanding and a huge comfort. They were remarkably mature. Their depth of perception has always impressed me, and I couldn't have hidden anything from them if I wanted to.

His surprise party stunned my Dad. Mum had sent him off on some trumped-up wild goose chase errand which gave us time to assemble the whole family and prepare the buffet. Dad arrived back about 5pm and we opened champagne. It was wonderful being surrounded by my family. For the first time in days I didn't feel alone. The champagne helped. We laughed and reminisced. It was a good party. I phoned the hospital every hour or so and still there was no change. By the time I went to bed I realised that I had left my overnight bag in the porch at home. So much for being super-efficient. I slept in Mum's spare nightdress (it would have made a good shroud), washed out my underwear and crashed out. There were just not enough hours in the night, I needed more sleep.

Sunday morning the kids and I were back on the road as soon as possible after breakfast, back to Leicester and another day in the hospital. Still no change in George but at least I finally got to meet the surgeon who had operated on him.

Mr. Tom S was of polish blood, I think, and apologies to him if I have got it wrong. He was young, handsome and very blond. Too young I thought. First sign of getting old when policemen and doctors look young!!! He had brought his little daughter with him on his rounds. She was like a little ray of sunshine, about 3 or 4 years old, with this halo of white blond hair. To the poorly, mostly older men in the ward she was the best tonic they could wish for. What a beautiful child!

Mr S took me aside and sat down to talk to me. He pulled no punches and told me exactly what the position was. George had almost died. If he had not been in the hospital when the heart attack happened, he would certainly have died. Only operating immediately had saved him. There would have been no time to call an ambulance, it all happened too quickly. He said that it had been the fight of his life to keep George alive. He said, "I fought him all the way. I am not sure yet what the outcome will be" he continued "he has two major problems now. The first is that we cannot keep his potassium levels constant and we want to keep him sedated as long as this is the case. The heart cannot function properly without the potassium level being correct. The second problem is that we do not know whether he has suffered any lasting brain damage as his brain was starved of oxygen because his heart would not function by itself when the by-pass machine was switched off. It was 45 minutes before the heart would beat during which time the team were desperately trying heart massage and any other measures to keep him alive."

There it was. The whole story of what had happened on Thursday morning. How could I not have known? I was cheerfully going about my mundane chores and I had no idea, no seventh sense, that this horrendous drama was taking place. I obviously have no extra perception skills or maybe after the years of medical crises, I had become desensitised to them. When I think back to some of the occasions when I have had to rush David into hospital with severe asthma attacks, I was always calm and detached then. Obviously, that is how I deal with emergencies? Some people panic, some are overcome with tears and emotion, I just carry on in a somewhat detached fashion. I am not cold or uncaring because I do not make a big display of inner feelings, its' just maybe that is the way I am and why I can deal with the situation and not get stressed. Many people have asked me how I kept going and carried on with running the home, family and business whilst all around me seemed to be mayhem, but to me there was just no other way.

Either that or I am just dense and unresponsive inside, desensitised and maybe a bit traumatised. Probably exhausted too.

RECOVERY, SLOWLY?

*T*he average length of time for patients having had bypass surgery to be discharged varies from person to person, but George took longer than most.

Following that dreadful Sunday afternoon, when I was finally given the facts of the situation, I must admit to some dreadfully selfish thoughts about my future. I drove home from the hospital that night and having dealt with the trivia of life, washing machine, unpacking from the weekend and the inevitable phone calls, I went to bed. For the first time I can ever remember, I could not sleep. I went downstairs and made a pot of tea in the middle of the night and talked over my future with the dog. Midge was curled up in front of the Aga (I think she was glued to it by the hip) and she let me rattle on for what seemed like hours. I have always talked my problems over with the dog. They love you unconditionally, listen and accept all you say without commenting and never answer you back. It is a most satisfying audience if you do not want an answer or second opinion. Seriously though, I was devastated and confused. The future was more uncertain than I have ever known it. I did not know if George was going to live (impossible to contemplate), and if he did, with what sort of quality of life? Was he going to be brain damaged and, if so, how disabled was he going to be? How was I going to support him, could I run the businesses and care for him as well? Would he be able to talk to me and was he going to be able to understand what I was doing or was he going to be trapped in a world of his own? If that was going to be the case it would have been kinder to have let him die. That thought brought me back to the unthinkable - and made me think. Then I thought, if he died, how was I going to be able to manage financially with all this building and bank overdraft hanging over me? It might sound selfish to even consider this at that moment, but it really was not, it was just natural to think about one's own self-preservation, anyway, even if it was selfish it was totally involuntary. After about the third pot of tea and day was breaking, I came to the conclusion that, as I wasn't in control of any of the above scenario's, the best way to deal with the future was just to take one day at a time, accept what the day threw at you and start each new day with a clean sheet. Otherwise I was going to become totally demented, imagining all sorts of dreadful things that may or may not happen depending upon the will of the gods.

So, although feeling exhausted, I tackled Monday with my new resolve and returned to the hospital. Gradually during the night, there had been some improvement and George was slowly being brought round. I sat by his bed and saw the first twitch of his fingers. The sister in charge of George was continuing this never-ending check of the drips, pulse, temperature, chemical levels and all the other associated tests. It was like perpetual motion, non-stop, round and round the bed. She must have the patience of a saint. She talked to him telling him who she was and what she was doing. I tried to talk to him too but I didn't really know what to say to him so I just burbled things like his mum sent her love and what the kids were doing (I didn't really know what they were doing because I hadn't had time in the last week to find out). I told him about

Dad's party and a load of trivial rubbish. Eventually his eyes opened. This was going to be the first test of any brain damage, recognition. They flickered open and closed for a few minutes whilst he came around and focused. Then the smile. The biggest grin you ever saw "Weewo" he said. I could not answer him. It was my turn not to be able to focus; the tears just streamed down my face. "Weewo" was what Oliver next door used to call me. Only being 2 years old, my name was a bit difficult to get his tongue around. As far as the rest of the Howard family was concerned that is who I became from then on and George had adopted it as a term of endearment. The tears of relief flowed on and off for the rest of the day. George didn't say much more as he'd got tubes down his throat, I managed to give him small drops of water on a sponge all day to keep his mouth moist and by 6pm I went home to rest. Next day there was more improvement and some of the drips were removed. Although still heavily sedated, some humour started to return, and he was trying to converse. He sounded quite drunk most of the time and slurred his words, some of them coming out backwards, but he was making progress.

After 5 days he had improved sufficiently and was moved from the ICU onto the surgical ward. He remained heavily sedated to allow his poor body to recover from the trauma. This meant that for the most part he repeated himself and didn't absorb what was told to him. I started to have to think for him, speak for him, make decisions about what he'd like to eat tomorrow etc. He did some hilarious things without realising. One evening he decided to go to the toilet. He could not get out of bed because of all the monitors and had a catheter attached. Not to be deterred, he reversed his bottom out of the bed, stark naked, with just a hospital gown, all the ties at the back undone. The man in the next bed was waiting for his by-pass surgery to take place and his wife was visiting him. She got a bird's eye view and with his rear fast approaching, she burst into hysterical laughter but managed to press the alarm button before he disconnected himself. They put the sides of the bed up then to prevent a repeat performance, but he just slung a leg over the bars and tried to do a western roll over the top. Paul, his nurse, and I had lots of laughs at his expense. Not unkind humour but a little bit of light relief during the critical time we had just lived through.

Every day there was improvement. Eventually he was well enough for visitors. His mum first. Amy was a tiny woman in her late seventies, very like the queen in looks and bearing. She might have been small in stature, but she didn't stand any nonsense. She'd had 5 children and George's dad had been a "Battle of Britain" RAF navigator so she'd dealt with her own stress in her younger days. She never showed much emotion, a family trait, obviously, but I knew how worried she was. She had lost one child; George's sister, had drowned as a little girl, and however much time goes by or how old you are, your children are always the most precious things in your life. A widow, she lived independently and would never ask for anything. She was most grateful for me taking her to see George. She didn't need to be grateful; to me it was the most natural thing in the world to take George's mum to the hospital first. She must have lived in a state of terrible anxiety for days with only my phone calls for news so when she saw George looking healthier than he had done for ages she was able to return home greatly relieved.

The reason that George had started to look so healthy was that he became jaundiced. He looked as if he had just returned from a holiday abroad, tanned and apart from the giveaway scars, looked great. I took all the kids in turn to see him and, because he looked so well, I think they thought I had been overreacting during the last couple of weeks. "Making a bit of a crisis out of a drama, were we, eh?" I got from John. Understandable really but I think they were also in a state of denial about their father's health. David and Alison understood. They had seen him the weekend of the party. Ann and John did not want to believe that their dad was very ill and seeing him in good humour and colour belied his real condition. I had learnt early on in George's illness that he put on a face for visitors and made light of the situation. When they had gone, he would complain that he was tired out and that it was my fault for having allowed the visitors in the first place. I told him to say that he was pleased to see them but please only stay a minute or two as he tired easily. No, he would never lose face like that, better to be brave and moan at me later.

After two weeks on the ward they still were not happy enough to let George go home but they really needed the bed for surgical patients. As George still needed treatment for jaundice, potassium levels and concern about his liver function they decided to transfer him back to our local hospital. He was taken by ambulance and the journey really upset him. It just showed how frail he was; he felt every bump in the road and was visibly shaking on arrival. He was put in the bed nearest to the nurse station where they could always see him and there, he stayed for a further 10 days.

He started to feel much better, confident, moaning

about hospital food and wanted to come home. I had to take curry, Chinese "take always" and all sorts of titbits into him. He had lost an enormous amount of weight and whatever food you gave him did not taste right. A man who previously loved his food was now picky and uninterested in meals. "I'll be fine when I'm at home" he kept saying." Elsie knows how to look after me". After his constant moaning, they allowed him to come home for the weekend. He had been in hospital for over 5 weeks and coming home was the most important thing in the world. I drove very carefully so as not to jolt him, and I had a fire laid in the lounge. I had chopped logs and shopped for his favourite food. A quiet few day at home to let him relax and heal. I was very edgy. I felt as if I was treading on eggshells. I am no nurse; I didn't feel confident about taking on the responsibility of caring for him. He was so frail, could hardly climb the stairs or dress himself. He was so anxious to come home that he hadn't realised there would not be any one qualified to nurse him. He came home on the Friday morning and by the end of Saturday he asked me to drive him back to the ward. He didn't feel well, he had a temperature, and I was at a loss. I was sure that if anything happened to him whilst he was at home, I would be blamed for it. Peter came and saw him and said that he simply was not up to coping with home either physically or mentally. He was scared and lost confidence in himself and I didn't have any to start with. Peter agreed with us both that he was better off back in hospital. It was noticeable that weekend that as George got more stressed, so his speech deteriorated. His words started coming out backwards again and his brain took time to assimilate questions before he could answer. This was obviously evidence of the brain damage and although sometimes this was a trial for him, he was so lucky that this was the extent of it. It also become a benchmark for me. If his speech started to go it was a sure sign of stress and overtiredness.

Disappointed with himself, we returned to the ward. He was in hospital then for a further two weeks before he came home again. It was by then the end of April and although still very cold, spring was on its way. The garden was full of bulbs and all in the world seemed to be coming alive again. What a long winter it had been. About 8 weeks after his bypass, George had to go to see Mr S for his follow up appointment. When we arrived at his consulting rooms, he got up from his chair and came round to the front of his desk and grasped George by the hand. He shook it firmly and said "I never ever expected to see you upright, George. How are you? He told us how he had fought to keep George alive and how worried he had been about the possible brain damage. He was amazed that George had recovered so well considering the circumstances. He also said that he had never seen such badly clogged up arteries in a man of George's age and that he regarded that operation as the challenge of his career. He told George that he was incredibly lucky to be alive at all and that he must slow his lifestyle down and eat a healthier diet from now on. "You have been given another chance, don't abuse it. The heart attack that you suffered was a massive one and you have sustained irreversible damage to your left ventricle. At the moment, we do not know how this will affect your day-to-day life, but you must take care of yourself. Do not over-exert yourself, get plenty of rest and try some relaxation techniques. It would be good for you to join the local rehabilitation programme and I will write this in my report to your consultant cardiologist." He continued with more advice for George and repeated several more times how amazing it was that George was alive. I think it really went home to George at just how close a call it had been. He was quiet and reflective when we went home.

We led a quiet life for the next few months, George would get up slowly in the morning, read a bit of the paper, go to bed for a few hours in the afternoon and watch TV before having an early night. His appetite returned and his weight increased. He looked better as his face filled out a bit. As the weather improved, George would have an afternoon snooze in the garden chair, well wrapped up. He felt the cold badly because he was taking Warfarin to stop his blood clotting. By the end of the summer he was almost back to normal. His scar healed well, and we even managed a few days holiday in Cornwall. We started to attend the rehabilitation programme at the hospital. A lovely girl called Yvonne ran the sessions once a week and we found them greatly beneficial. I especially enjoyed the relaxation held at the end of each week. Based loosely on Yoga relaxation, I would be asleep by the end of the session, the most wound down in the class, and I was the only one that hadn't had a heart attack! I was sorry when the programme ended. Yvonne, previously a ward sister, worked for the cardiology department. She was extremely helpful, and George gained a great deal of confidence from her. He could ring her up for advice and she was always willing to give her time to listen and advise. George and I found her much easier to communicate with than the consultant whom she worked for.

THE CONSULTANT CARDIOLOGIST

I knew that, by reputation, he was a highly qualified consultant cardiologist now retired. I am not throwing any doubts about his abilities as a doctor. He ran an incredibly busy department and with the number of patients suffering from heart disease of one kind or another, his workload must have been astronomical. After the early years and traumas of George's condition we were referred to Dr. C after we expressed dissatisfaction with the previous cardiologist, he sent George off immediately for an angiogram; so we thought he was wonderful. Three months after Mr S transferred George back to the care of the local hospital, we went back to see Dr. C. He was most impressed by Mr. S's surgery and reports of George's condition and continued the treatment with a combination of pills. Warfarin to stop any clotting, beta-blockers and lots of other Latin named pills to control different aspects associated with heart disease. We were again on a learning curve. Some of the pills helped, some definitely did not. One product, the name ended in 'pril' gave George a terrible cough. It racked his poor chest, which was already painful enough, having been opened up during the by-pass surgery. Anything prescribed with 'pril' at the end had the same effect. It was apparently one of the side effects of that product, but it made George suffer dreadfully. Eventually, by a process of elimination we found this out and our GP suggested George try an alternative.

Every three months we had to see the consultant during the first year and thereafter every six months. We found that the appointments became more and more of a chore. Whatever time we were due at the clinic so were about 20 others, like a block booking. You could guarantee at least a 2-hour wait and has been as long as 4 hours. Dr. C was always late starting his clinic, he had been called out on an emergency, he hadn't finished his ward rounds, or he was in a meeting. There was always an excuse/reason. The NHS lack of cardiologists was just as bad back then as now and their workload immense. By the time George had been for blood tests, been weighed then waited to be seen, it was a day's outing. If, when you had waited all that time, you managed to talk to a doctor, it would have been worth it. No, you were whisked in, another doctor looked at the notes, muttered a few trivialities, sometimes their English was good enough for you to understand, most times you could not, and then you were out. You were in and out so fast that the questions that you wanted to ask were forgotten in the rush and you wondered why you had bothered. It was very disconcerting. If you are faced with an illness like this, you feel constantly at a loss, you are not in control and therefore, you are relying on the experts to help you understand what you are facing. You need their support and time. Time is something the National Health Service does not have. There simply is not enough time in the day for every patient to have 5 minutes to discuss his or her own particular circumstances and concerns with the consultant. To be fair to the doctors on the team, they were working flat out. They were probably hearing the same story repeated and as a result they become de-sensitised to the individual. But for every single one of those patients, what had happened to them was totally devastating, to their immediate circle of family and friends, and the only person qualified to help with their ongoing treatment was that doctor in the clinic. So, we felt somewhat at sea. Nobody really to talk to, nobody to reassure you when you lose confidence in yourself and nobody to tell you what is happening to you. Again, to be fair, is that the job of a doctor? We decided that we needed to find out as much as possible about heart disease, its' causes and consequences for ourselves so I read everything I could lay my hands on and asked advice from our GP.

Our GP, Dr. Freeman, was our lifeline along with Peter. The doctor would call in periodically on his way home from surgery. "Just to say Hello," he would say. "I was just passing and thought I'd pop in." He would listen to George's chest and just watch his colour and breathing. He just kept an eye on him really. Peter would call round, or we would see him in the garden and again, he just monitored him.

We had several occasions to complain about the Cardiologist's clinic and the delays. On one particular day, we sat for 3 hours in the clinic until 5.30 (appointment time 2.30pm). The receptionist asked about 20 people if they would like to rebook their appointments as she was going off duty. Most of the patients grumbled but grudgingly agreed. George did not. He had been anxious to talk to Dr. C and refused to leave. He got quite worked up about how inefficiently the clinic was run and said that if he had run his business in that haphazard way, he would have been bankrupt years ago. He felt that it was appalling to book 20 people in all at the same time – did they think that all these people could afford to take an afternoon off work and sit there for hours and then be told to rebook. I got incredibly angry because George was obviously stressed, in the very place that was supposed to help. In the end we did leave but I wrote a letter to the chief executive of the hospital.

When I started to add up the problems that we had had over the years, I became terribly angry indeed. If George had been properly cared for after his first two heart attacks, he would have been given an angiogram. This would have revealed that he had 3 blocked arteries, which needed surgery. This surgery is now so routine and successful that George possibly would have had no further problems. He could have continued his business through to retirement and not have needed any more help from anyone. The fact that the consultant failed George was bad enough and it took advice from Peter to tell us what we needed and resulted in us having to make a fuss with the GP to persuade him to refer George for a second opinion.

The resulting delay meant that George had a third and fourth heart attack and a near miss emergency by-pass. Because the surgery was undertaken in a crisis situation meant that it was much more dangerous, and the fourth heart attack had caused the left ventricle to be severely damaged. Why does the National Health Service have to delay situations so that it ultimately costs far in excess of what the initial treatment should have been? Crisis management is what it is, and it appears to be endemic.

So, I put my case in a letter to the head of the hospital with a copy to our GP and a copy to the Cardiology team. This was nothing personal, just a statement of facts.

I received a reply 3 or 4 days later. It was a polite letter to say that they were sorry that we felt we had cause to be dissatisfied with the treatment and George was to be offered an appointment with the Consultant himself to discuss the situation. It was one of those standard letters with no real sympathy, just platitudes really.

However, George did get another letter from the clinic and we were summoned at 9am the following week. I was taking bets with myself as to how long the delay in starting the clinic would be and I was pleasantly surprised at only 20 minutes. We barely had time to drink the coffee that I had purchased in anticipation of a long wait. No reference was made to the letter of complaint, no apology for the abortive appointment and Dr. C was still not keen to discuss any aspect in great detail. In fact, his opening words were "I have to be in a meeting at 9.30am" i.e. make it brief. This time, however, George was not to be deterred. We had made a list of questions and systematically worked through them. The doctor had obviously never encountered anyone like George before and was caught off balance by his direct approach. He was used to calling the shots and did not like being questioned. We persevered and just about dragged answers from him. His secretary interrupted to say his meeting was due to start but George didn't waver. "I'm sorry Doctor, but I haven't quite finished yet" was George's response. In the end the doctor was 10 minutes late for his meeting and we felt that we had got our point over. It was a feeling of great personal satisfaction that we had at last had an exchange with the man, but at what cost. George had asked him some direct questions like "what was the prognosis for his condition to improve. Was there anything further that could be done to improve his health?" The answers were fairly short and concise, economical with language to be exact. The top and bottom of it was, we learned, that George's heart was failing, the damage to the left ventricle was severe and he would slowly, gradually, get weaker. His shortness of breath would get worse as his heart function deteriorated. The pills he was taking would gradually be less useful and there was not much more that could be done. It was the way it was, and we had better get used to the idea that that was it. He said that a heart transplant would probably be the eventual solution but there were many patients in the same position and very few transplants available. He had nothing else to offer and nothing else to say.

To a lesser mortal that would be pretty devastating news, barely 50 years old and not much to look forward to. George, in characteristic fashion, was not taking that lying down.

BAD TIMES

*T*his is a chapter that must be included but not one to dwell on. As you can imagine the prognosis given to George was bound to make life difficult to cope with. Whether it was the pills he was taking that made him so bad tempered, the situation, fear, jealousy at my seeming good health, frustration, facing your own mortality or a combination of all these factors, life with George became a nightmare. When I woke up and said, "it's a lovely day" George would say it wasn't. If I said, "this colour was white" he would declare that it was black. It didn't matter what I said, he would contradict me. Suddenly everything that had happened to George was my fault. "I didn't have a heart condition before I met you. It is you that have caused me all this stress".

There is no greater, lethal combination than financial instability, being bad tempered, at odds with your wife and denial of your ill health all at the same time.

This situation went on for a long time, during which we moved house, selling our barn to help repay the bank, we wound up the car business completely and dealt with the ongoing enquiry (more like the Spanish inquisition!) from the VAT (HM Customs and Excise) as previously mentioned. I went back to work as well to help with the financial crisis. Talk about stress on top of stress on top of stress.

I kept saying to myself that George was only saying these horrible things to me because he was so ill. He cannot mean them. I was trying to do as much as possible to relieve the stress but was ending up making things worse. You can only keep going for so long before you start to believe what is being said. He was verbally so abusive; I was F.....g stupid, "Shut up you don't know what you are talking about, can't you ever do anything right, you spend too much, don't use 2 tea bags to make a pot of tea, its wasteful, you don't cook a casserole like that." (I cooked a boeuf bourguignon for dinner with friends one night; it needed long, slow cooking in the Aga and steeped in red wine. I went out to the shops to pick up a few last-minute goods and when I came back George announced that the meal was tasteless, I was a useless cook, so he had added some curry powder to it!) it tasted awful and ruined what should have been a lovely supper with close friends.

I spent a lot of time in tears trying to analyse and understand the situation and make allowances for it. Outwardly, I am an extremely confident, gregarious, fun loving person. Capable and competent. Inside I am not sure of myself and so when you are constantly told you are stupid, an idiot and useless, then you start to believe it. Undermined, to that extent, I allowed myself to be controlled. Our sex life totally disintegrated, and I was blamed for that as well. For anyone reading this, it is important to realise that when a man's heart does not work properly, then the other parts of a man's body do not work either. The heart is what pumps the blood round! I don't need to be any more specific, do I?

Eventually, and inevitably, I snapped. With the benefit of hindsight, I am surprised it took so long before it happened. No warning, no pre-planning, I just lost the plot. I woke up one morning, came down to get breakfast whilst George opened the mail. The bank statement had arrived, and as usual George went ballistic about the state of the overdraft and as usual it was my entire fault. I just looked at him, calmly got up from the kitchen table and very quietly and slowly said. "Enough, if all your problems, both health and financial, are my fault, if I go away then you won't have any problems anymore. Simple." I went upstairs and packed my clothes, loaded all my personal belongings in the car and drove away. George watched me, stunned at how calm I was, no histrionics, almost zombie like. It wasn't till I had driven out of the village that I suddenly wondered where the hell I was going to go.

David was at University and Alison was at college and they shared a flat in Nottingham by this time; I arrived on their doorstep later that morning. Not exactly what students expect or had bargained for but obviously I was made welcome. I was devastated that for the 2nd time in my life I had failed in marriage, exhausted from the pressure of the past couple of years but feeling guilty at leaving George when I knew how ill he was. I simply could not take any more. It was a sort of breakdown – I just had to get away before my gaskets blew. This was, I think the lowest point for me. Now we have a situation called "Coercive control" which is now recognised as grounds for divorce and a huge cause of mental illness. I had no idea of this at the time, I just felt drained, empty, a total failure.

My kids were wonderful and supportive. They instinctively knew that I was close to collapse and just welcomed me in. I was incapable of decisions, drifting, thinking id get another job locally, a flat, I'd been on my own before so I could do it again. Inside though I knew that despite everything, I really loved and cared about George and knew that without me he would struggle to cope. My brain was everywhere. I was at that point absolutely mentally exhausted. I tried to keep on working but my mind was really not focused. One very upsetting incident happened whilst I was staying at the kids flat was that one day, whilst I was out at work, Ann turned up at the flat. It was very strange as Alison said she had never been to visit before. She said that her dad had sent her to pick up the jewellery that he had bought for me, my engagement ring, wedding ring, a pair of diamond earrings that he'd given me for my 40th birthday present and Rolex watch. Alison said that I always wore my jewellery so there was nothing in the flat and even if there had been, she would not have given it without my say so. Ann left after that as she realised she wasn't going to get what she was after. Alison rang me at work to tell me as she thought it very odd. Furious, I immediately rang George to give him an ear bending, and I asked him if he had indeed instructed Ann to do that and he denied it vehemently. Said no, he would never ever do that, and he was obviously very upset at what Ann had done. So much so that at work the following day, I received a huge bouquet of flowers saying how sorry he was, and please would I meet him to talk, which of course I did. We met at a local restaurant for dinner and it was like being on a first date again but despite how much I cared, I knew I needed some time out. I couldn't live in that powder keg again. So we agreed to separate whilst we each worked things out. We both knew that we loved each other but the stress of the past couple of years was more than I could cope with.

I was absolutely hopping mad with Ann and decided

that it was a deliberate case of attempted theft. She had taken it upon herself to try and steal my jewellery, she was so jealous that George had bought these things for me. So for the second time in my life I wrote a very strong letter to her and a copy sent to her mother saying that if I ever found out again that she tried to steal from me, I would report her to the police. What she had done was appalling.

I could go on and on about me but that is almost another story in itself. This tale is about George and I must get back to the point. Sufficient to say that I stayed away from George for 11 months, getting a flat of my own, which I hated, losing my job because I was unable to function properly and so I went to live temporarily in Bath with my brother and sister in law. Eventually, because of the verdict on George's health, I came out from under my cloud of self-pity and I went back home. George was at first outwardly reluctant to have me back but deep down he was hugely relieved. As it turned out, if I had not left, George would not have gone to America and the outcome of this saga could have been vastly different.

So, traumatic as life was, it could have turned out even worse. Sometimes life just happens for its' own reasons which we are not privileged to know at the time.

GEORGE'S BEST FRIEND BILL

*B*ill had been a best friend of George's forever. They had known each other for about 30 years, ever since they met through motor racing which was long before I knew George. He would retell some wild and wonderful times they had together. Bill had owned several businesses in Luton. He subsequently sold out and made a modest fortune.

When George and I first met in 1988, he took me to Mijas in Spain to introduce me to Bill. He had moved out there after he sold his company and lived in this lovely villa high in the hills behind Fuengirola. The views were wonderful, and we spent a happy holiday with Bill and Jean. I remember being very envious of their lifestyle. Money no object, no demanding kids, just a calm life in a lovely climate and environment. Not long after, the exact date I cannot remember, Bill and Jean sold that house, moving to the Isle of Man. It was Bill and Jean's wedding that George went to when I took the kids to Spain on holiday just prior to heart attack no.3. Some while later, Jean hated the cold, wet weather after the Spanish climate, and so they moved again, this time to Sarasota in Florida, and we went to stay with them again. The house was magnificent, the weather was great in the winter, too hot for comfort in the summer but with air-conditioning, I understand that you get used to it.

I have mixed feelings and emotions about Florida. I love the warmth, the sunshine and the wildness of the thunderstorms. I love the long golden beaches and the feeling of being on the edge of a dangerous, vast swamp with all the wonderful wildlife, that the cultivated parts would be swallowed up by the swamp if unattended for long. But I get bored with the flatness, the sameness and the unending roads of billboards and tacky stores. I loved Disney Land, Sea World, the Epcot Centre and Universal Studios. Pure fantasyland. I loved the Space Centre and best of all Busch Gardens. I enjoyed that most and would go back tomorrow. We have explored both the east and west coasts. We loved the fresh fish and generally the food is amazing (and loads of it)!!

When Susan and George were going through marital problems George went to stay with Bill in Spain and so it was almost inevitable that when we separated that George would seek some solace and TLC with Bill again, but this time in Florida.

My story here might not be quite in chronological order, but you will have to forgive me, as I wasn't actually there. I was back in England, living with my kids in their student flat, trying to get my head straight.

George went to stay with Bill and Jean as I said for some TLC and had 2 or 3 weeks there. He relaxed and gained benefit from the warmth, sunshine, distanced from the stress and enjoyed the friendship. Bill introduced George to an acquaintance of his, a nurse called Peggy. George told Peggy the whole saga over the next couple of weeks and took quite a shine to her. She turned out to be a nurse who specialised in the care of heart patients and so was able to give George a lot of advice about his condition.

She found it hard to believe that George had been allowed, under the British National Health system, to have 3 heart attacks before being sent for an angiogram.

THE PLOT

*B*ill decided that George needed to take some fairly drastic action about his medical condition. Fuelled with the information from Peggy, they discussed what to do next.

George knew that he did not have time on his side. Peggy had already said that he could get some medical advice in Florida, a second opinion would at least help him to come to terms with his situation but the cost of medical care in the USA without insurance can be prohibitive.

"What about holiday insurance. If I were taken ill and rushed into hospital as an emergency, what treatment could I expect?" he thought at least it was worth a try.

So, George came home, but he kept in touch with Peggy. She gave him a lot of encouragement and advice over his diet to help control his high cholesterol level. He started to do some research into travel insurance and hatched a plan with Bill. Some months later he arranged another trip. He got a flight to New York. He stayed there for a couple of nights, having a little adventure on his own. He managed to scare himself in Chinatown in some seedy nightclub; the grim details of which he never told the whole truth about, and then caught a bus to visit some mutual friends of ours who live in a little place called Owega in New York State. George did not realise just how big a place New York State is and was on this bus for hours. He had left a message on Ray and Laverna's answerphone to say what time he was arriving. He got off the bus, late at night, as he said," in this one-horse town with the tumbleweed rolling down the road". He watched the bus drive away and he was totally alone in the middle of nowhere, knowing no one. I think George felt at his most lonely, low and vulnerable at that point. 5 minutes later however, car headlights appeared over the horizon and Ray arrived to rescue him. Thank goodness.

He spent a week or so relaxing with Ray and Laverna, but snow was falling and the temperature freezing so he decided it was time to go to Florida, the sunshine and to hatch the plot.

After a few days recovering in Florida with Bill and Jean, regaling them with his adventures in New York and his marathon bus journey across the USA, but actually having scared himself witless and feeling very fragile, he renewed his acquaintance with Peggy, and it was time to test the system and the insurance.

Bill phoned the emergency number 911, said a friend staying with him from the UK was feeling ill and thought he might be having a heart attack. Within seconds the ambulance, together with a fire engine, arrived (apparently in the USA they always travel together). These great big burly guys came into Bill's immaculate home, all marble floors, white leather sofas and fur rugs, did some preliminary tests and whisked George off to hospital. Within minutes of arriving they did an angiogram, decided that in actual fact he had had another, though mild, heart attack, not surprising with the stress of the planned subterfuge, and did an angioplasty immediately (where they insert a balloon into a blocked artery to inflate it).

Why can't they do that in UK?

However, the verdict was not good. The news that the

doctor gave to George was pretty devastating. This recent event + 4 previous major heart attacks, by-pass surgery being done too late, all had so severely damaged his heart, his left ventricle in particular, that he gave him between 12 – 18 months left to live if he did not have a heart transplant.

At this point Peggy said she would introduce George to a colleague of hers who was a transplant doctor. Not a surgeon but a clinical professor and the best in the field.

Peggy wanted a second opinion from someone whose judgement she trusted. This news was something that you did not mess about with and there was to be no delay.

PROFESSOR GUILLERMO (G)

$\mathcal{J}$ ust a little background to this amazing man. Small of stature, wiry and of Puerto Rican background. He stands about 5 feet 5 inches tall, swims every day of his life to control his asthma, eats anything – his wife Mary Anne (MA) wonders how he hasn't killed himself from food poisoning, incredibly intelligent, articulate, amazing memory, avid reader, loves art galleries, museums, history, architecture – and racing cars. Oh joy. A soul mate for George.

Peggy arranged for George to meet him. Known generally as G. She gave him all the hospital notes who confirmed the prognosis. He told George that, as he had control over where the donor hearts were given in South Florida, he could arrange for George to go on the transplant waiting list. BUT. The cost of medical treatment in the USA is astronomical and with no national health scheme to speak of it would cost George about 200 thousand pounds initially for the surgery but the ongoing costs for the rest of his life would be prohibitive. George would not get any insurance and he would have to move out to Florida permanently to qualify to be accepted on the list. Basically, G told him that he could not afford to do it. It would take every bit of money he had and then some. George was, by now, much more financially stable, the worst of the recession being over, and the properties sold. However he was at that point facing the possibility of a divorce looming between him and I. His solution was that he was going to a world heart transplant conference in Miami within a couple of weeks where there would be several British representatives attending. He said that George's best option would be to have the surgery back in England if he could get him onto the list but told him that he would absolutely not be accepted if he was going through any marital problems and advised him to sort himself out. With all due respect, George did admit to G that our separation was mainly his fault and that he had driven me away with his dreadful temper and attitude. He knew I was devastated, and that he was to blame.

What would George have done if he had never met G? I often wonder. I can say with almost certainty that this story would have had a vastly different ending.

The two of them got on like a house on fire, went to some American race meetings together over the next couple of weeks and started to forge the friendship that has lasted ever since. Since then we have returned to Florida several times to holiday and always to stay with G and MA. They have turned out to be exceptionally good friends indeed and someone that I could always ring to ask for advice about George, get reassurance and a straight answer.

I digress. George came home to England. G went to the heart conference in Miami where he met a doctor from Harefield Hospital, Middlesex. He introduced himself, gave him George's file and said "You should see this guy. He seems to have slipped through the net of the National Health System in the UK, he needs a heart transplant and fast".

Refresh yourselves back to chapter 9. After 11 months of living apart, Mandy and Peter, who had kept me informed throughout about George's health, rang me to tell me that George had been to the USA and was told he needed a heart transplant but, going through a marital separation and domestic disruption, was not likely to be accepted onto a list. He needed to be in a stable relationship as so much depended on domestic harmony and help together with family support. This devastating news was what brought me out from under the cloud of despair and I immediately returned home a week or so after George had returned from the USA. I had never stopped caring for George, but he had made my life a living hell and I needed us to be apart, but when I knew he would not get the chance of being accepted onto the transplant list without me, there was no choice or second thought. George made a big show of reluctance to let me back into the house but, in reality, he was hugely relieved that I was home. He had to face so much, the prognosis was not good and at that point he was no nearer to getting a transplant and was back in the dubious care of the National Health System. Not much to give him hope or confidence after his previous experiences. He was scared as would any of us be, faced with his future. After all the grief of the previous months, it took a while to settle back into a normal married life. I said to myself, but never to George, that I would stay with him to give him the best chance of getting the transplant and look after him till he was OK but if his attitude and temper, downright unreasonable behaviour, didn't improve, I would have to leave again, I owed that to myself, my dignity and wellbeing. but I could not see him deprived of the lifesaving surgery because we were separated. I had never stopped loving him but just had not been able to live with him, his bad temper, verbal abuse and unkindness. Big deep breath and keep your temper, agree with everything George said, just keep it all together and try to get his health sorted out. It was just vital.

We decided to have a holiday to try to put ourselves back together again. In George's mind, holidays were where you took yourself away from the daily routine and gave yourself time to talk, relax and recharge. Even though he had not long returned from the USA, he needed to face his demons, coming to terms with the reality of his health situation and we were both in need of rebuilding our relationship. As it was April and not yet very warm, we chose to go to Tenerife. Some mutual friends recommended a good hotel. George's daughter Ann was working in Tenerife at the time so we thought it would be good for George to catch up with her as well. So, we booked a holiday and looked forward to some peace, tranquillity, sunshine and some much-needed time on our own to repair our much-damaged marriage and my bruised and battered self. Oh how I wished for that.

COINCIDENCES

*T*he day before we went on holiday, we learnt, quite by accident, from mutual friends, that George's ex-wife had also decided to go to Tenerife to see Ann. Six weeks previously her boyfriend had tragically died whilst they were travelling to Australia for a holiday. As you can imagine, she had had a very traumatic experience. They were supposed to be having the holiday of a lifetime, but he fell ill on the plane as they approached Singapore airport. He was taken straight to hospital where they diagnosed a ruptured artery in his heart, a condition he had been nurturing all his life but knew nothing about, and which killed him within a matter of hours. Obviously, she was devastated and after the funeral decided to get away to the sunshine for a complete break. We had never been on the best of terms as you will remember from earlier chapters, but I did feel sorry for the situation she had found herself in and felt the best thing to do would be to phone her, which I did. It turned out that not only were we going to the same island, we were travelling on the same flight and we were staying at the same hotel. Inwardly I groaned (and I expect she did too) and wished I was going anywhere else in the world but there. Sometimes you have to ask yourself if life is just testing your ability to cope and how much you can deal with before completely cracking up.

The idea was for George and I to have some private time together, for George to deal with the psychological effects of his medical condition and for us to learn to live together again in peace and harmony; to make the most of what life expectancy George had. It would also have been nice for George to have some time with Ann on his own. Now I was faced with dealing with our delicate relationship, George's daughter and his ex-wife all at the same time and in the same place. I really did not know how I was going to deal with all this. I desperately needed some space and peace in my life, and I had an awfully bad feeling that I was not going to get it in Tenerife. Anyway, there was not much I could do as we were flying the following morning. I thought that I would just have to make the best of it. My nervous breakdown would just have to wait a little while longer. Gird your loins, Elsie and grin and bear it.

We all met at the airport and were polite to each other, we even had coffee together and talked about what a shocking coincidence this was. When we boarded the plane, we found the situation almost hysterical; whoever was responsible for the seating plan had decided to seat us all together in one row, the past and the present wives, together. It was obviously someone with a great sense of humour or a diabolical mischief maker. Fortunately, we saw the funny side (or was it a case of minor hysteria), particularly George whose old sense of humour returned and thought it hilarious. So during the four-hour flight we got on remarkably well. The greatest relief was to find that at the hotel our rooms were a long way apart.

At dinner that evening George and I relaxed over a lovely meal and several glasses of wine. The hotel was lovely, our room had a balcony overlooking the sea, the food was excellent and we started to relax and appreciate each other's company, We agreed that we had really missed each other during the separation and now valued it even more, we decided that come what may, despite the obvious curved ball we had been thrown with the "ex" intruding into our private time, we were going to enjoy our holiday and make a determined effort to save our marriage.

At the other side of the very large restaurant, however, we could see Susan sat, dining all by herself. She looked a very small, sad, lonely lady. George and I agreed that we could not leave her sitting by herself all night and so we asked her to join us for coffee and a nightcap, on the terrace after dinner. That set the pattern for the holiday, we just couldn't leave her on her own, she appreciated the company and I think it helped her come to terms with her grief, Ann enjoyed seeing both her parents together and although the situation was bizarre, we all managed to enjoy the holiday.

In a lot of ways, I think it helped us all in the understanding of our relationship and it eased the tension that had existed between us. I have to say that it caused great amusement amongst our friends at home and has been a situation that we have laughed about many times since.

Sometimes you must question what the master plan for life is, how I was meant to cope with all this, what my final breaking point was and what a crazy life I led.

THE WAITING GAME

*O*n our return from Tenerife we had a telephone call from a doctor at Harefield Hospital, Middlesex, who sounded quite confused. He had been given George's medical file at the heart conference in Miami and could not understand why a doctor had referred a British patient from Florida and not from a UK Cardiologist. So, he was anxious to meet George to find out what was going on. This was our first journey to Harefield and as it turned out, one of many, many journeys to come over the next years. This first appointment was to assess whether George could be considered for a heart transplant. This meant going through a whole series of tests both medical and psychological. It was also designed to test whether or not I was up to the job of being partner, nurse, wife, friend, support and the many other attributes needed to cope under the circumstances. We quickly learnt that there are very many patients who desperately need a heart transplant but never even get to be put on the waiting list. The number of donor organs are so few and the number of patients so great. The tests to get on to the waiting list are rigorous as they must be very sure that the recipients will be able to cope with the ongoing treatment for the rest of their lives. It isn't just having an operation from which you are going to recover, it is the beginning of a life dominated by pills, endless check-ups, hospital treatment and altogether a whole new way of life. And so, we returned home to await the initial assessment results. We waited several weeks and eventually heard that

George was to go to Harefield for three days of intense medical tests before being considered and if regarded as suitable, subsequently, accepted on to the waiting list.

George was incredibly nervous, also extremely excited. It was like we had been looking down a long black tunnel and suddenly seeing a chink of light at the end. We also knew that it was still going to be a long journey to find that light and that it was uncertain that we would even get there. We went to Harefield. George went through all these tests I spoke to nurses, psychologists, sisters, doctors, anaesthetists and other patients who had undergone heart transplantation. Those three days showed us that our life was going to change, and you become part of the Harefield system.

We returned home knowing that it would be two or three weeks before we would have the results of the tests. It was the most nerve-racking experience of our lives. It was like waiting for school exam results, your future was going to be shaped by the outcome. We were both walking on hot coals around each other not able to deal with each other's feelings because we were unable to deal with our own. All the previous trials and tribulations, difficulties and problems with our lives paled into insignificance with the enormity of what was to come. If George was accepted on to the transplant list it still was not certain he would ever get a heart, he was a rare blood group, which made the odds even longer. Just an aside, George, as a racing driver, had "O" blood group embroidered on his racing overalls as a requirement. If he had ever had an accident on the racetrack and had needed a blood transfusion, it would have killed him. I asked how he had found out that he was "O" blood group and he said he hadn't, he'd just guessed!!! He wasn't "O" at all but "A"! Typical George who made up his own rules!

If he did not get a donor heart his fate was sealed and if he did get a heart, there were no guarantees that it would work anyway. Damned if you do and damned if you do not. How did we deal with it? You just do - and we did. Sometimes I think that it brought us closer together, but sometimes we were so rattled that we could hardly be civil to each other. We began to understand why the tests were so important because the stress upon each other was so great that they had to be certain that you are strong enough characters to live with this. It was most certainly the greatest test of strength of character that I know of or have ever had to go through. Perhaps all the testing times I had been put through previously was my training ground for this and for the future? Who knows?

Knowing that we had a two-week interlude we were advised to go away for a holiday, so we decided to do something we have never done before and go on a cruise. Once you are actively on the transplant waiting list you cannot go any further away than a two-hour drive, at any time, from Harefield, and you have no idea how long the wait will be. So we knew that in future, foreign holidays were going to be out of the question. We thought that this would be quite an adventure and something quite different. So off we went. We flew to Barcelona where we joined the ship and had a wonderful week cruising around the Mediterranean. We met a lovely couple from the USA, Eddie and Roberta, who I have stayed in touch with all through the years. It was the beginning of November so, although the weather was cool, the sun shone most of the week. We went to

Venice. Sailing in at dawn, past the entrance to the Grand Canal on a ship that is taller than the buildings was quite the most incredible sight I have ever seen in my life. This was in 1996 and since then the damage and pollution these huge cruise ships have done to Venice have made the cruise companies change the way they approach the port, but back then it was just an incredible experience. In Sicily we became involved in a national disaster as a torrential storm had washed away part of the road, stranding us at one end of the island and quite unable to get back to the ship for many hours. Because of this disaster the ship was unable to leave on time and as many of the passengers had been involved in the trauma, the captain decided to stay in Sicily for an extra day. We had been due to arrive in Rome on Saturday but arrived instead on Sunday. We employed a taxi driver to drive us around Rome and show us the sights. It is a wonderful city; the ruins of the Coliseum and the many other ancient buildings and monuments were spectacular. The taxi driver took us to the Vatican City arriving at 11am just as the Pope appeared to address the crowds. St Peter's Square was packed, and we were right at the back. We could see a tiny figure far in the distance dressed in green. The Pope. I have never been a particularly religious person. I attended Brownies and Sunday school as a child, married in church – twice - and went to funerals, christenings and weddings and occasionally at Christmas, but not what you would call a regular churchgoer or with any deeper religious convictions. However, I felt at that moment a desperate need to ask for help. I don't usually pray but I figured that if there really was a god then at least the Pope was nearer and closer to him than anyone else, so I said a few quiet prayers asking the Pope to put in a few good words for George. It couldn't do any harm, could it, and we needed all the help we could get? Who knows whether it did any good, I'd just like to think perhaps it did? I certainly felt that we were meant to be there to see the Pope and if the disaster hadn't happened in Sicily, we would have missed this incredible experience.

I believed it was meant to be.

Well anyway we had a wonderful time and arrived back home to find a letter from Harefield saying that we had been accepted for George to go on to the transplant waiting list. We were issued with a bleep each, which we always had to carry, day and night. We both bought up to the minute new mobile phones and learnt to leave messages wherever we went so that we could be traced in minutes if a heart organ became available. We packed bags with essential toiletries, pyjamas and a spare set of clothes so that when the call came, we could leave immediately. That was in November 1996. Christmas came and went as did January and February. At first the waiting was nerve-racking and then just when we had almost forgotten about it there was a phone call in March, we looked at each other almost in disbelief, then huge smiles of relief and off we went. I have never seen anyone so looking forward to having major, monumental, surgery. George was so elated, he wanted to drive himself there, but I thought his blood pressure might not be worth the risk, so I drove. He was more animated, livelier and humorous than I had seen him for a long time. We arrived at Harefield in plenty of time and quickly became involved in the routine of preparing him for surgery. What seemed to be hundreds of blood tests were taken, he was showered, and shaved, dressed in hospital gown and paper knickers and it was all overly exciting. The anticipation and atmosphere was electric. After all the preparations were complete George climbed into his hospital bed to wait for the pre-med injection. We were told we might have to wait an hour or two. We waited for four hours, by which time it was past midnight, then a doctor came to tell us that the donor heart was no good. He was deeply sorry to bring us this bad news, but they did not want to risk giving George a heart that was less than perfect. We did not have any idea how devastating that news was going to affect us. We were totally unprepared for that result. It was like having all the air let out of all your tyres, all at once, disappointment and disillusionment fell around us there. It was 1 o'clock in the morning and although we were tired, we decided to go straight home. I felt so, so empty I could hardly speak; the following day George felt so exhausted and dejected and we both had a severe sense of humour failure. You cannot begin to describe how totally drained and flattened we felt. All the hope and the anticipation of the previous day just destroyed. It took several days for us to come to terms with the disappointment and get over the sense of loss. It was real grieving. But like everything else and in life you get over it and you get on with the business of living.

That was our first major setback, but we carried on. April, May and June passed. Then we got another phone-call. We felt that it was George's second chance and we were off to Harefield in a flash. Exactly the same procedure as the first time took place and then we sat again for several hours waiting for the moment to go to the operating theatre. And again, we were told that the heart was damaged and therefore the surgery would not go ahead on this occasion.

The disbelief that this could happen twice! I felt that my strength of character was being pushed beyond the limit and I wasn't too sure of how much more we could take. This time we were too devastated to drive home, and so we slept at the hospital and drove home the following morning almost unable to speak. I have never been a depressive sort of a person or one to get down in the dumps about things. I have an incredibly good sense of humour and am normally able to bounce back but this time I was about as low as it is possible to get.

How George dealt with this disappointment I do not know but his strength of character is obviously more resilient than mine.

A NEW PROJECT!

*I*t was an average sort of summer, but it was quite obvious that George was becoming weaker and weaker and found everyday tasks increasingly difficult and tiring. It took longer for him to get up in the morning, having a shower and a shave took so much energy from him that he had to rest after breakfast. He would potter about the house unable to raise much enthusiasm to do any jobs and what jobs he did tackle exhausted him. He usually went to bed for couple of hours in the afternoon which gave him enough energy to cope with the evening. He was almost always in bed by 10 o'clock and slept through until about nine in the morning. He was sleeping more and more and being awake less and less. I became more worried that by the time a heart was found that George would be too weak to cope with the surgery.

I can remember, like everybody else in the country and probably in the world, that terrible morning in August when we woke up to the news that Princess Diana had died the night before in a tragic road accident. We grieved along with everyone else in the world and I think, for the first time, I let go of some of the grief I felt inside for myself. Until then I had not shed a tear or allowed myself to feel sorry for myself or for George and the situation he was in. He was only 52 and we both felt that it was unfair that he should be facing this when he should be looking forward to grandchildren and retirement. But then Diana was much, much younger than George and she didn't get a second chance either.

Several weeks before Diana's terrible accident, George and I had been out for a drive and we took a detour up a little country lane near the canal to look at a house, a whole farm in fact, totally derelict. I could imagine it two hundred years ago, its' beautiful Georgian facade, ornamental garden, pond, together with its' own well and all the old farm buildings. What a history, what a story this place had to tell. George had known the children of the farmer 25 years ago and it was here that George first became interested in motor racing and built his first racing car along with the farmers' son. This is where the motor racing bug bit him and it became his lifelong love and ambition. I looked at George and thought to myself, he wants to buy this to renovate. He must be stark raving mad in his state of health to contemplate a monumental project like this. The house was huge and the surrounding barns enormous, but with so much potential. I could almost see the cogs turning in his brain, and the pound notes in his eyes. He looked at me and said, "what do you think". In that moment I realised that this would save George's life. He would have something to aim for, a dream to achieve, taking him back to where he began almost but with the drive and desire to bring this wreck of a place back to its' former glory. Part of his apathy was that he was bored, had nothing to occupy his brain, nothing to strive for. Without any hesitation I said, "We'd better buy it then" and then thought "you're as barmy as he is".

We went home and rang the estate agent to put in a stupidly low offer, half the price it was advertised for and I thought to myself that we would never get it for that price. We sat and added up, almost on a scrap of notepaper, how much money we had got and how much it would cost to rebuild and renovate. We both knew, having had lots of previous experience in barn conversions that whatever you budget for, it always costs double.

Work colleagues of mine were going to a wedding near to us, so we let them have our house for a few days and swapped our house for theirs in Brighton, still only 2 hours away from Harefield and armed with our bleeps in case the call came. It would be a change of scenery and a breath of sea air. We could only talk about this project. Whether or not we could afford to do it, would George survive it, were we completely mental to even consider it? We enjoyed 2 days of sunshine, sat on the seafront at Brighton, discussing this monumental decision and then it started to rain. We decided to come straight back home to get a final answer from the agents. We were too excited and energised to stay away. So, home we came; to our astonishment our offer was accepted so, excitedly, we started the planning process, which became ongoing for months. The price was agreed, the loan in place to fund it; we were set to buy Lowes Farm. Even though George was weak and could not work for long, his brain was racing. Exchange of contracts was set for November 5th, Bonfire Night! How apt!

My Mum and Dad had decided to move from Hertfordshire to be nearer to me, well in fact I had suggested this to them saying that with a sick husband, I couldn't really be travelling 2 hours to them if they needed anything as they got older. They quickly found a house nearby, their house in Hertfordshire sold really quickly and they moved on, guess what, November 5th, 1997. A day to celebrate. Our first granddaughter arrived on my birthday, November 10th and that same week I went out to buy a dog. We needed a deterrent as the farm was uninhabited, up a deserted country lane and there was going to be lots of building materials arriving and left unattended. I visited the local RSPCA and found 2 of the most ferocious looking animals I have ever seen. Bess and Marnie crossed Belgian Shepherds with I'm not quite sure what else. Big, black, hairy monsters. They scared our team of builders half to death when I arrived at the farm with them, big burly guys scuttling up ladders or into vans, but they turned out to be the softest, most gorgeous 8 legs you could ever imagine. Perfect for scaring off intruders but lovely company with beautiful characters. With Dad now on hand to help out, we went to London to see Ann and the new baby on 17th. I thought to myself, whilst driving back from seeing this lovely little bundle, that November had been quite an eventful month so far and with completion set for December 5th, I had much to think about and plan for.

Amongst all this excitement I was also trying my damnedest to work. I was at the time working for a wonderful Medical Research charity as a professional fundraiser covering all the East Midland counties, a very large patch with quite a considerable amount of travel involved. Whilst it was supposed to be a part time job, it was also very demanding. The Charity held its' annual conference in London on the 27th November and I had a lot of preparation to do so the next few days were spent on getting my presentation boards done. I had a "one to one" meeting booked with my area manager on 26th at a local hotel near to home. Do not ask me why I packed my presentation in the car and took it with me to the hotel.

Premonition, I don't know? I said to my boss, as we were concluding the meeting over a cup of tea at 4.30pm, "I wish that George would get his new heart soon as he is becoming ever weaker, despite the energising effect the prospect of the new project was". I was beginning to think that it really would never happen and that I would be left with this enormous development of ten barn conversions to develop by myself. Fiona, my boss, said that she hoped that it would come soon as well and that I was not to worry about work - she would cover for me and I was to take as much time off as was needed. At that precise moment, my mobile phone rang. Fiona said, "I'll get the bill for the tea as I must get off to London to prepare for tomorrow's conference and I don't want to get stuck in the traffic". I said, "I bet that's George on the phone wondering how much longer I'm going to be and what's for dinner." It was George. "Get home ASAP - Harefield have just rung we've got to go - and now". Fiona and I ran to the car park - I bundled my presentation boards into her car and drove home like the wind.

The 2 previous occasions we had gone to Harefield had been full of anticipation, calm but hurried. This time was different. I was not mentally prepared - I had too many other things happening in my brain, that I was no longer focused on the most important task. I should have been catching the train to London the following day to the conference. I had been so busy getting my presentation ready that my bag for Harefield wasn't packed properly, I was flustered and rushed.

It was a horrible November evening, the worst kind. It was dark, miserable, windy, and cold so we drove in blinding rain, heavy traffic on the M1 because it was 5pm and neither of us really believed it was going to happen; having been let down twice you do not let yourself hope. It took over two and a half hours to get there but we had rung them to let them know we were on our way and were at the mercy of the traffic and the weather. We were both frazzled when we got there as you are after a dreadful journey. I wanted a cup of tea and something to eat as it was after 8pm and I had not had lunch due to my meeting. I thought that George's blood pressure would be sky high after that drive, mine certainly was!

*I*t was exactly the same procedure as on previous visits but somehow there was a greater sense of urgency, a more positive feeling. We had arrived just after 8pm, by the time George was prepared and ready it was 10pm. I spent quite a while on the phone making domestic arrangements - letting all the kids know where we were and George's mum too. Arranging for Mum and Dad to look after the dogs and our house, the builder who was securing the farm gates prior to the major building work commencing and all the other things that had to be dealt with. Clearing the decks, you might say, trying to put our house in order. Oh what a time to be contemplating the biggest and most dangerous surgery possible!

I drank coffee, found a stale sandwich in a vending machine and we sat down to wait. George, of course wasn't allowed to eat because of the impending anaesthetic. By 11.30pm I was beginning to think - here we go again. They will tell us soon that we can go home, thinking that with so much going on at home, it would almost be a relief. Then suddenly, a doctor came in followed by a porter with a trolley, loaded George on and down the corridors we went. It happened so quickly that neither of us realised what was happening till we got to the operating theatre doors. George said "I'll see you in the morning, Weewo. Bye". The heavy black rubber doors to the operating theatre swung open and he disappeared from sight.

I stood at those doors for …. I don't know how long,

seconds probably but it seemed like hours. I can't tell you how I felt because it was indescribable. Like being in a dream, almost like it was not really me standing there; what am I doing here; what do I do now; where shall I go; this isn't happening to me; this is not real? Then it hit me, like a train smash.

The whole sheer enormity of what was going on the other side of those doors. Someone has tragically died tonight in order for George to have this operation. Someone's family are distraught and torn apart by their death and George is being given their heart.

Heart - what is it - it's your life source - so many parts of the body you can live without - people live with only one lung, one kidney, one eye, one leg - but your heart - you are nothing without it. Vital, essential to life. Who was the poor donor - how did he/she die, why did he/she die? So many questions, all with no answers.

I suddenly realised that George was in there having his chest cut open and his own heart was being taken out of his body; if this failed there would be no going back, no more chances, this was it. Life or death, I might never see him alive again.

So many things left unsaid. So much unplanned and so unprepared.

Then the tears came. They were involuntary and unstoppable. I think about 5 years' worth. They just poured out of my eyes and my knees finally buckled. I was still standing facing those doors when my legs gave way and at that very moment the Sister from the transplant ward, happened to walk past the theatre on her way for a much-needed coffee break. She caught me as I went down and helped me to her office a few steps away. All the emotions, fear, terror more like, pent up from years of George's illness, marriage strains and putting on a brave face. We British and our stiff upper lips. Maybe if I had shown more emotion before it would not have been so bad. It was, I know, it was a pressure valve blowing but I was inconsolable, uncontrollable tears just poured out. Sister Alice poured coffee into me when the sobbing finally subsided. We sat and talked for hours - till 4am. She was wonderful that night and I will never forget her kindness ever. Eventually she told me to go to bed as I would need to be strong in the days to come and that I must get some rest. I had a room booked in the hostel adjoining the hospital. Despite the amount of caffeine, I had consumed, the exhaustion took over and I slept till 8 am.

NOVEMBER 27TH, 1997, GEORGE'S NEW HEART'S BIRTHDAY

At 8 am. when I woke up, I felt guilty because I was supposed to ring at 7am to see how he was doing. I should not have worried because he was still in the theatre and no one could give me any news. So, I showered, washed my hair, dressed and went to find some breakfast. Isn't the human body amazing? After all the trauma of the night before as soon as I walked into the hospital canteen and smelt bacon, I was ravenous. A hearty breakfast later I went across to the transplant ward to see Sister Alice. She had gone off duty and would not be back till the evening. So, I wandered aimlessly waiting for some news, which finally came about 10 am, when they had him back to the ICU from the recovery ward.

He was attached to a bank of monitors, which looked a bit like Cape Kennedy. Pipes and tubes were inserted into every orifice of his body and quite a few extras as well. He was a ghastly colour and unconscious. He looked dead, other than the whooshing sound of the machinery, which indicated a steady regular heartbeat and therefore proved that he was alive. I was able to speak to his surgeon a while later who assured me that it was not an easy operation and he had given cause for concern several times during the procedure. Read into that what you like but I think he had a very tough time. His potassium levels were not stable (what's new, we've been there before) but his new heart was functioning well. Mr K, the surgeon, explained in minute detail what he had done. It was quite revolutionary. George had a high-pressure reading in his own heart and lungs, which was going to make it difficult for any new heart to cope with. He had been given the heart of a young man who suffered from cystic fibrosis and whose heart was used to dealing with high pressure. Mr K had left George's own heart in place and inserted the donor, and smaller, heart in the right hand side of his chest going in through the rib cage horizontally instead of vertically through the breastbone, therefore not disturbing the existing bypass grafts from several years previously. So, George now had 2 hearts beating happily away inside his chest. I am still totally amazed, even now, when I think about the sheer skill of the surgeon. What an incredible man, what a lovely man, what an amazing man to have that sort of skill and ability. I have been in total awe ever since.

What then emerged was even more staggering. The young man who had given George his heart was still alive This is the part that I cannot, and probably never will, get my head around even now. Tragically, a young girl had been killed in a motor accident, we believe in Wales. Her tissue type and blood group matched that of the boy in the Royal Brompton Hospital in London. A cystic fibrosis sufferer, he desperately needed a lung transplant. Apparently, back in the 1990's, it was then easier to perform a heart lung transplant because of all the interconnected blood vessels, than just the lungs. The recovery was better, and the operation was more successful. So, he was transplanted with the heart and lungs of the young girl, his own lungs were just thrown away but his heart, which was fine and strong, and a tissue and blood group match exactly for George, was sent by helicopter from the centre of London to Harefield Hospital and given to George. If that isn't one of the most amazing thing you have ever heard of, I don't know what is. If ever there is a case for compulsory organ donations, then this is it. Whoever the young man is, who received her new lungs and heart, I hope he is still well and enjoying life to the full.

Our eternal gratitude is to the grieving family of the young girl who so sadly died and is without doubt the most overwhelming emotion. I hope that her family can take some comfort and pride in the knowledge that she gave at least 2 people a chance to live. There are no words in our language that can be used to describe the gratitude and put a value on the gift that she gave that awful night. She gave the Ultimate gift – LIFE. Who could ever repay that? We do not know who it was and are never likely to know. But the enormous debt of gratitude we owe to her will never be forgotten.

Mr K wanted George to be kept under anaesthetic for the rest of the day to allow his body to recover a bit more, so I made the phone calls to a very thankful and relieved set of kids, relatives and friends. Obviously, all the kids were genuinely concerned and the first call that I made was to George's mum. Amy was beside herself with worry although she would never have let me know it. I phoned America to G and Mary Anne. G came on the phone and wanted to know all the intricate details of the surgery. Mary Anne said that as it was Thanksgiving Day in the USA, she had been to church and said a little prayer for George. She said, "God was listening to me, yesterday wasn't he?"

I wonder. Did the Pope relay my prayer; did he listen to Mary Anne? I do not know but I would like to think so. My religious belief is sketchy at best, tested further when, feeling so emotional and for once in my life I felt the need to say a prayer, I went to the chapel within the hospital grounds. I think I wanted to feel a sense of hope and maybe find some peace, but the doors were locked. A sign on the door said to get the key from reception but the moment had passed. It didn't matter, I was happy with my hope that the Pope had heard me together with Mary Anne's faith and accepted without questioning.

So, I sat by the bed all day watching the monitors, George totally motionless. If his chest hadn't been moving with the help of the respirator you would have thought he was dead: He looked lifeless. There was nothing there - no movement, no personality, nothing. I should have felt elation, happiness, he had come through it, but I felt extremely low and very depressed. I had no one to share my anxieties with, no one to talk to about what was happening, I just sat there, holding George's hand, waiting. Eventually tiredness took over, mental exhaustion more like, so I said to the sister on duty that I was going to bed and to ring the room if there was any change. She said that they were going to start to bring him round in the morning. I fell into bed about 9.30 pm and slept like the proverbial log. It was with absolute horror that I realised in the morning when I woke that it was already 10 am.

NOVEMBER 28TH

*D*ay 1 of the rest of our lives. Learning to live with a heart transplantee. What lay in store for us both? We had lots to find out.

I rushed into the ward - no time for shower or breakfast this morning.

"Weewo (George's pet name for me) where have you been. I've been waiting for you for hours" was yelled at me as I went through the doors of the ICU. George was sitting up in bed, still a ghastly colour, but grinning like a Cheshire cat. "I've got a new heart" he shouted at the top of his voice "I love Mr K, he's a wonderful man". I had to agree and laugh at him. I don't know what they were giving him through those tubes but often there have been times since when I would have liked some of it. He was on Happy Pills, Cloud Cuckoo Land, away with the Fairies, not quite on this planet but hovering above it. Aware of his surroundings but definitely in LaLa Land. By the end of the day they had to move him out of ICU, back into the Transplant Ward but in a private side room because he was making so much noise!

That was in 1997, it has taken until 2020 for the organ donation laws to be changed. As of this spring, it is to be assumed that unless you have opted out, then you have consented, by implication, that your organs can be used for transplantation if, sadly, you die. It is a very controversial step and some people will find it difficult to accept. I believe though that whatever your religion and belief, the opportunity to give someone else the chance for life outweighs the objections. There are those who would not want to donate their organs but would be happy to accept a transplant if they subsequently needed one. That to me is a hypocritical attitude although I know that there will be many who disagree. You must be in the situation we found ourselves in to maybe understand the desperate need for organ donations, kidneys, heart, liver, etc.

RECOVERY

For a couple of days George remained on this amazing "high". Then gradually they weaned him off the drugs – and reality began to take hold. The family were, of course, anxious to see him. They all wanted to see him as soon as possible. His mum was first. I had to drive up to Derbyshire to collect her, drive to Harefield, in Middlesex, a 2-hour drive, then allow her about 20 minutes visiting, then drive her home and then return myself, a 9-hour round trip. That was exhausting in itself, 8 hours on the M1 and M25! Then son John, daughter Ann, who was cross at not being able to bring the new baby. Strict instructions from the doctors that new-born babies were not allowed to see new transplantees for risk of infection due to the patients' non-existent immune system. Try explaining that to both Ann who insisted her father would want to see his new granddaughter, and George who said he wanted Ann to bring her into see him. Neither could, nor would, seem to understand the reasoning behind the rules, so I, of course, as usual, was the bad guy, the bossy britches, the kill joy! Then David and Alison, George's brothers, sister, cousins, racing friends all wanted to visit. I had to make a rota and make them stick to it for fear of tiring him. Then, as today, hand washing was compulsory before entering the room. If any of them so much as sneezed, they were refused entry. Any colds, coughs or any possible infections were banned. I had to allow them only a few minutes at a time and only one visitor per day. He was permanently exhausted. It was like running a military operation. Flowers arrived by the boat load, but they were not allowed in the room as the infection risk from the vase water was very high. Any little task was taxing, and progress was terribly slow. Sometimes it was one step forward and two steps back. The pill regime was frightening, the anti-rejection drugs, the side effects, rashes, allergies, sickness, diarrhoea, hallucinations, irrational temper. Getting the balance of pills is so vital to recovery and the realisation that these pills will have to be taken at regular times every day for the rest of your life. Life took on a different meaning, priorities had to change, and you are absolutely tied to the pill regime. No deviation as to times and dosage. You had to plan ahead to make sure you never run out, have duplicate sets of pills when travelling in case the pill bag goes missing or is stolen. Learn a whole new way of life. Cleanliness, hygiene, everything had to be sterile, the risk of infection and subsequent rejection, was a constant battle. Phew!

You know just when you think that life could not possibly throw any more at you to deal with – it does.

Remember I told you earlier that we had bought Lowes Farm (chapter 15) as a new project. Well, we had exchanged contracts on November 5th as arranged. Mum and Dad had sold up and moved from Hertfordshire to be nearer to me, settling into a nice house in a neighbouring village. Completion of the purchase of Lowes Farm was set for December 5th. We had already started work, making the site secure and getting plans drawn up, architects, planning applications and schedule of works, builders and a whole host of other jobs lined up and ready to go. Normally after exchange of contracts, the completion goes through without any hitch. Not this time, I could have put money on that, couldn't I? I kept getting phone calls from our bank manager. This was difficult as my mobile was switched off all day in the hospital so by the time I picked up the missed calls it was after 5pm and so didn't manage to speak to him for about 6 days. Eventually I got hold of him and he was really quite rude. "I need to speak to George urgently, I need him to sign some documents before completion can take place" Bear in mind the time scale. George's surgery was on 27th November, I had missed calls for 5/6 days, so it was about the 2nd December when I took this call. "Where is George, I must talk to him?" "He's in London" I replied, "what is so urgent?" I didn't want him to know where George was or what had happened for fear that he got cold feet and pulled the plug on the massive bridging loan he was giving us for this project. Who would loan half a million pounds to take on a monumental job like renovating 9 derelict barns and a grade 2 listed Georgian farmhouse to someone lying in a hospital bed, having just undergone heart transplant surgery and unable to even clean his own teeth? George had never admitted to the bank manager that there was anything wrong with him, let alone tell him he was on a heart transplant waiting list. I knew I just had to try to fob him off and not tell him the truth or we would be in very deep, extremely hot water. So, I drove from Harefield hospital in Middlesex to Derby to collect the documents for signature, drive back to the hospital, get George to sign them and then drive back to Derby. Ok I thought job sorted. I stayed overnight at home, the first time I had been home for nearly two weeks, I could not face the trip back again in one day. Then the bank manager rang back the following day "I just need one more signature". I exploded at him. It takes a lot for me to lose my cool but boy, did I lose it then. I told him, in no uncertain terms, that all these documents should have been signed before exchange and that it was his gross negligence that these signatures had been missed. To which, surprisingly, he admitted that I was right and apologised profusely. I then told him where George was and why. I said I am not doing the same round trip of over 600 miles that I had done the day before, that I was coming down to the bank and that I would sign them. "Do you have a problem with that "I said. He said he would ring back in a couple of minutes. I think he needed to catch his breath, have a coffee (or maybe something stronger) and a cigarette and work out the consequences. He rang back and agreed that it was in order for me to sign for the loan to go through. That was fortunate as the following day was completion. December 5th. Phew.

I must have nerves of steel, where I got all this strength from, I will never know. Only I knew that my knees had turned to complete jelly!

I spent the next couple of weeks, quietly, at George's bedside writing Xmas cards and sending a (hateful) pre-printed letter about George's progress to all our friends and relatives. It was realistically the only way that I could inform every one of his progress. I went into nearby Uxbridge shopping and managed to buy all the kids a xmas present, wrapped everything and loaded them into the car, not knowing when I'd next get to see them but at least everyone had a gift. My brother bought me a spa day in London at the Sanctuary. Oh, how I needed that. It was wonderful, lovely swimming pool, steam bath and a seaweed slime bath, needs to be experienced once in your life; after a 45 minute soak, steeped in green, gloopy slime, you then stand naked in a shower tray and are jet hosed to remove the green stuff which by that time had stuck to every possible nook and cranny of your body! Nice! My skin, however, felt amazing afterwards, just soft and wrinkle free. Very lovely relaxing day.

During the month that we were there, George slowly started to get stronger, his scars healed remarkably well, the pill regime became more routine and his body got used to them, so the side effects diminished. We did have some fun and games with him though. He had regular hallucinations and bad dreams, sometimes I would go into his room in the morning and he would be fast asleep because he hadn't slept all night. Sometimes he was wide awake having slept well but in a terrible temper, no reason for it but just that the world was a dreadful place for him at that moment, sometimes frustration at his inability to be normal, sometimes fear of the unknown, fear of the future, how to cope with a second heart pumping in his chest, the fear of it stopping. One evening, just before xmas, I went to the dining room for my usual meal and returned to the ward about 7pm to tell George that the dining room was all decorated with garlands, the Xmas tree was lit up, the staff were having a party, and everyone was singing carols around the tree. A lovely evening. I regaled all this and then thought nothing more about it and went off to bed. At 2am, my mobile phone rang; it was the doctor on duty saying could I come over to Georges room as he was in a bit of a state. The hospital hostel for guests is about a 100-yard walk from the main hospital, set in the woods. At 2 am it was a bit unnerving to be running around in PJ's and dressing gown, in the cold and damp, December night. Anyway, I got into the ward to see the doctor and a couple of nurses barricading Georges' door. George was shouting at the top of his voice, he wanted to call the police as the staff were out to murder him, only I was allowed to go in, only I could help him." Weewo, you've got to help me escape, they've been plotting all evening in the dining room to kill me, they've been singing about how to kill me. I've got to get out of here, I've got the builders in at home and I need to get out now". I tried extremely hard to explain that the staff had been singing carols, no one was plotting murder and that the doctors were there to help him get better not plotting anything sinister." He was bouncing in and out of the bed, quite deluded. I said to him we just all wanted him to get well and we were all trying to help. "Aaha", he said," so you are in league with them as well, you are plotting to kill me too, well I'm going to get you first" and he lunged at me clutching the bedclothes. At that moment, the doctor and nurse burst into the room, grabbed George and stuck a hypodermic into his thigh. He dissolved almost immediately onto the bed, zonked out, not sure what they dosed him with, but it worked. It was quite scary to see him so violent, so wild eyed, so totally obsessed but so deluded. The following morning, he was as bright as a button, back to normal with no recollection at all of the night's events. We laughed about it many times later when I reminded him of the night. Fortunately, although he had some awful dreams, nothing as bad as that happened again. That was a scary one.

The day before Xmas eve the doctors agreed that George could go home till after Boxing Day. I rushed off to the local

Marks and Spencer's in Uxbridge and bought, quite literally, Xmas in boxes. We drove home, on Xmas Eve, slowly, as George was very uncomfortable, and I think very scared too, with the car laden. Finally back home, I helped George to bed then unpacked the car. On Xmas day there was a tree, decorated, turkey, Xmas cake, and mince pies, crackers – the whole works. Alison was the only one of the kids who came home – the others had obviously not expected us to be home and had made other arrangements. She was amazed when she arrived that the tree was up, "how did you do all this Mum, what can I do to help". "Just open boxes," I said. And we did – everything was in an M and S box. Turkey, trimmings, roast potatoes, brussel sprouts, gravy, cranberry sauce, xmas pud, brandy sauce, presents for everyone and a couple of bottles of champagne, which Alison and I shared. I have to say that after years of knocking myself out to make Xmas cakes and puddings, peeling mountains of veg and spending the better part of the day cooking it was quite a revelation to just open boxes. The most taxing part of the day was getting the timing right – we just cut out the cooking time labels from each box and laid them out in chronological order on the work surface. What a laugh it was – a sort of hysteria, I think.

After 3 days of being back home, we were back to Harefield on 28th, then allowed home again for New Year, back to Harefield on Jan 2nd. This became the pattern for the next few weeks, my little car knew the route down the M1 and M25 so well it almost drove itself. In between all this I was going up to Lowes Farm to give instructions to the builders, paying their wages, ordering the materials, making decisions I knew George would hate and trying at least to keep my own job ticking over. My boss was so understanding and gave me a 3 month leave of absence to get my life back on track. I had almost forgotten that I had a demanding job too. How I didn't lose weight is a total mystery to me! Not that I was fat but just astonishing that the scales never altered. I never stopped from November 27th, 1997 to March 1998 only to sleep for about 6 hours a night. Backwards and forwards to Harefield, learning to manage the pills, managing a building site, 3 dogs and George's irrational temper and frustration.

God bless my mum and dad, my kids and friends.

All the time I was tearing about like a man possessed, a whirling dervish, going in ever decreasing circles, George's health gradually improved, and his physical ability progressed a little at a time.

HOLIDAY

*I*n March, the doctors decided George and I could go away for a few days for a much needed break and he did not have to report back to Harefield for two weeks. Freedom from the M1 and M25 for 2 whole weeks. Wow!

In years past, George and I used to go to the Lake District from time to time and had learned to sail on Lake Windermere. Such lovely breaks we had enjoyed in the fresh air. So, I booked a small motorboat on the lake, packed the car with hot chocolate, soup, porridge, bacon, eggs and beans and all the warming foods I could. Sweaters, boots, hats and gloves loaded, we headed off. Fresh mountain air, wonderful scenery and total isolation. Absolute bliss. The first morning we sat, wrapped in dressing gowns, on the deck of the boat, steaming mugs of tea, and looked at the snow on the mountain tops. Although very cold, it was sunny and crisp. A day that I remember as being a turning point. Possibly because it was the first time, I had allowed myself to stop and relax for months, take stock of the situation we were in and begin to hope that it would all be ok. As George was still far from well, but on the road to recovery, we couldn't sail, it would have been far too strenuous hence renting a motorboat, but one day we decided to go up the lake to a favourite restaurant, for a trip then have lunch. I took the helm of the boat but as we approached the jetty to tie up, I let George take the controls whilst I jumped off to secure the rope. Strict instructions to come alongside very slowly then put the engine in reverse as soon as I jumped off the side, so we didn't hit the jetty. Hmm. It was still very much winter, and the jetty was very wet and slippery. I jumped off, landed on the jetty, slid straight across and plunged into the lake the other side. George was able to secure the boat by himself and I managed to climb out of the lake, up the ladder but of course I was drenched and frozen to the bone. The owner of the restaurant saw out of the window what had happened and rushed out with towels and wrapped me up. On a tiny boat there were very limited washing and laundry facilities, so the hotel owner took me inside for a hot shower and provided us with a splendid lunch and dried all my clothes. What we hadn't realised till later, was that the hotel and restaurant were still closed for winter and wasn't due to be opened till Easter. Such a kind man and an absolute godsend. Just another adventure to recall with laughter.

I have often wondered how I am not a total basket case!!!

Slowly, slowly over the rest of 1998 George grew stronger, threw himself into the renovation of Lowes Farm, the House itself, the Farmhouse at the rear and 8 further barns to convert, eventually moving there permanently at the end of the year. So, year 1 of the transplant was achieved with no major hiccups, no periods of organ rejection.

A monumental triumph really.

ell we have had some ups and downs over the past 9 years. I gave up trying to do another job as I allowed my better judgement to prevail. I am not a Nicola Horlick who can do everything. I am fallible and not super woman – I still try but not with as much conviction as I used to.

George and I finished the development of Lowes Farm with all the properties sold. We lived in the farmhouse and although we talked from time to time about selling, I still loved it there and felt as if it is where we belonged. There are always finishing off jobs, landscaping and maintenance but essentially, we had retired.

George had a few bouts of illness, was still susceptible to chest infections and picked up bugs and anything going around, but, as his immune system was very compromised it was only what was to be expected.

The worst scare we had was in 2004 when travelling to Florida to see our old friends, G and MA, our wonderful heart doctor without whom George would never have survived. George was suddenly taken ill, would you believe, on Thanksgiving Day, the anniversary of his transplant, and was rushed into hospital where he was diagnosed with septicaemia. Where he got that from or how, we will never know. It very nearly killed him but somehow, he fought back and survived yet again. Once again G took charge of the treatment plan at the hospital, our insurance company flew a doctor out to Florida to escort us back home. I was left to pack up all the luggage, deal with the return of the rental car and get myself to the airport. The insurance company were wonderful to George but not to me, I just was left stranded to sort myself out. I finally got to the airport where George and the doctor had checked in, first class of course, I had all the luggage and found that I was put into a cattle class seat with no frills, no access to the first class lounge where George was until a very kind lady at the check in desk took pity on me. I think my harassed look made her help. She upgraded my ticket and sent me off to join George. When we boarded the plane, the doctor was busy wiring George up to the oxygen supply, he was in a bed and she had the seat beside him. I was put into an adjacent seat and the Stewardess looked at me and quietly said "would a glass of champagne help" I politely replied "Oh yes please, and can you set up an intravenous drip for me so that the glass remains full the whole way home" My glass was never empty that day. Bless her heart.

That episode reminded me never to become complacent about George's health again.

George's greatest pleasure became spending time at Silverstone where he was a member of the British Racing Drivers Club. He loved to go to the clubhouse during the racing season to socialise with old colleagues and former rivals from his racing days. They would discuss the politics of the club, reminisce over the old days when racing drivers were made of sterner stuff than today. I called them a bunch of old "has - beens" – to which the reply came back "better to be a "has been" than never to have been a been at all". How very true.

END OF PART ONE

I cannot finish this part of the story without mentioning the unknown person who made all this possible. To say, "thank you", could never be enough. What happened nearly 10 years previously shows the amazing capacity of strength that we humans find in our darkest and most desperate hour of grief. That the family who donated their daughters' heart and lungs could think of others at that time still astonishes me. I only hope that they can take comfort in the fact that she helped, probably many others as well as George, as she died. Her life was most certainly not in vain.

To the amazing people at Harefield Hospital where we spent so much time, the Transplant team of surgeons, Sir Magdi Yacoub, who performed the Lung Transplant surgery at Great Ormond Street Hospital, known to the Harefield staff as "God 1", Mr Asgar K, the surgeon who performed Georges' surgery and known affectionately as "God 2" and the entire Transplant Clinic team, such wonderful people that to say simply thank you, never seems to reward their incredible dedication and achievements. You will never be forgotten.

When we used to register our wish to be an organ donor, we never even consider the real implications that one-day we might have to fulfil that obligation.

With the new laws on organ donation coming in 2020 it is a wonderful time to reflect on the true meaning of what it is to donate an organ. So many people need a kidney transplant, so many need a liver, heart and other organs too. Although the cost of this amazing surgery is vast to the NHS it is nowhere near the cost of keeping patients on dialysis and the lives of hundreds of people who die just waiting for a transplant with all the associated human grief and suffering.

Organ Donation - It is the Ultimate Gift - Life

Although I have come to the end of the story about our experiences of heart conditions and Organ Transplantation, with all the ups, downs and traumas we lived though at the time, this most certainly isn't the end of the saga. What came after is almost stranger than fiction. As friends have said to me on many occasions "you couldn't make this up, you need to write a book about this". And so I have.

The sequel "The Aftermath – the Ultimate Survival" completes the tale by bringing us right up to date in 2020.

Lightning Source UK Ltd.
Milton Keynes UK
UKHW011827221020
372056UK00002B/109